Praise for *Brilliant, Crazy, Cocky*

"Anyone who thinks they know entrepreneurship should read Sarah Lacy's *Brilliant, Crazy, Cocky*. Being an entrepreneur is about thriving in chaos, and you will find chaos—and great opportunity—in the emerging world right now. Yet for all the talk about the emerging world, only this *Brilliant, Crazy, Cocky* brings you a true-to-life account of the on-the-ground struggle to create something huge. In this engaging read, Lacy will change the way you see the world. Anyone with a pulse should read this book."
—Marc Andreessen, partner, Andreessen Horowitz Ventures; co-founder, Netscape, Opsware, Ning

"Part insightful analysis of what ails Silicon Valley and part madcap journey to far flung hubs of aspiration and innovation, Sarah Lacy takes us around the world to find the fascinating people who are creating the new wealth in a new world of start-ups and ventures that America ought to be paying a lot more attention to."
—Maureen Orth, special correspondent, *Vanity Fair*

"Sarah Lacy's entertaining and informative tour of the world's fastest growing economies undeniably proves what we've known at Endeavor for more than a decade: impressive and inspiring entrepreneurs can truly come from anywhere! In taking us on a whirlwind journey bursting with frenetic energy—matched only by that of the amazing entrepreneurs she meets—Lacy gives us an important glimpse into the future of the global economy—a place where the craziest, high-impact entrepreneurs—from anywhere and everywhere—set the pace."
—Linda Rottenberg, co-founder and CEO, Endeavor

"Sarah Lacy has focused on a fascinating phenomenon and explains, with clarity and unimpeachable logic, why and how these global entrepreneurs are saving the planet. Everyone interested in what makes the world spin better must read this book."

—William H. Draper, III, co-founder, Draper Richards LLP
Author of *The Startup Game: Inside the Partnership Between Venture Capitalists and Entrepreneurs*

"Entrepreneurs advance human welfare by creating the economic future through the messy process of starting and growing companies. Sarah Lacy has seen this future and, in this essential and important book, chronicles the emergence of a new, global era of messy capitalism. The critical question Lacy poses to the United States and other countries is whether they will join this entrepreneurial revolution or watch it from the sidelines."

—Carl J. Schramm, president and CEO,
Kauffman Foundation

"*Brilliant, Crazy, Cocky* puts a well-deserved spotlight on the fascinating entrepreneurs working in some of the most overlooked places on Earth. This book reminds us that when entrepreneurial opportunity is enabled and embraced locally, the economic and social benefits have the power to transform us all."

—Pierre Omidyar, founder and chairman,
eBay; founding partner, Omidyar Network

BRILLIANT, CRAZY, COCKY

BRILLIANT, CRAZY, COCKY

How the Top 1% of Entrepreneurs Profit from Global Chaos

SARAH LACY

WILEY

John Wiley & Sons, Inc.

Published by John Wiley & Sons, Inc., Hoboken, New Jersey.
Published simultaneously in Canada.

For general information on our other products and services or for technical support, please contact our Customer Care Department within the United States at (800) 762-2974, outside the United States at (317) 572-3993 or fax (317) 572-4002.

Wiley also publishes its books in a variety of electronic formats. Some content that appears in print may not be available in electronic books. For more information about Wiley products, visit our web site at www.wiley.com.

Library of Congress Cataloging-in-Publication Data:

Lacy, Sarah, 1975-
    Brilliant, crazy, cocky: how the top 1% of entrepreneurs profit from global chaos / Sarah Lacy.
        p. cm.
    ISBN 978-0-470-58009-7 (hardback); ISBN 978-1-118-00778-5 (ebk)
    ISBN 978-1-118-00779-2 (ebk); ISBN 978-1-118-00780-8 (ebk)
        1. Entrepreneurship. 2. Success in business. I. Title.
    HB615.L23 2011
    658.4'21—dc22

                                                                2010034717

Printed in the United States of America

10 9 8 7 6 5 4 3 2 1

To all the brilliant, crazy, cocky entrepreneurs in megacities, slums, and villages around the developing world. You've inspired me more than you will ever know. And for my husband, Geoffrey, who supported this brilliant, crazy, cocky journey.

Contents

This book was made possible by a grant from
the Kauffman Foundation.

ACKNOWLEDGMENTS

*M*y first thanks have to go to John Wiley & Sons, Inc.—the only publisher that would take a risk on this book two years ago. The second thanks go to the Kauffman Foundation, who made the reporting financially possible without my going bankrupt. Thanks also to Michael Arrington and TechCrunch for the steady paycheck and platform to write about my journeys as I experienced them. Thanks to my agents at Levine & Greenberg, who never made me feel crazy for taking this project on. And thanks to the publishers who *did* make me feel crazy, because you pushed me harder.

I spent 40 weeks on the road for this book, and it's impossible for me to thank everyone within each country for his or her translation, hospitality, trust, and honesty. In Israel, thanks to Roi Carthy, Michael Eisenberg, Yossi Vardi, Erel Margalit, Gilad Japhet, Orli Yakuel, Ayelet Noff, and the amazing staff of the Hotel Montefiore in Tel Aviv for being my surrogate Jewish mothers.

In China, thanks to Peter McDermott, Richard Robinson, Yang Cao, Liam Casey, Na Chai, Jeff Xiong, Song Li, Gary Wang, Kaiser Kuo, Gang Lu, Kai-fu Lee, Yan Zhang, and Roy Ho among many, many others. An especially huge thank you goes to Tom Limongello, who traveled with me and translated during my first trip, and to the Opposite House—the single best hotel I stayed in during my travels.

In India, thanks to Naren Gupta and the staff of Nexus Venture Partners for letting me crash in their office space, to Vishal Gondal for taking me to my first Indian cricket game, and to Abinash Tripathy for nursing me back from Delhi Belly (Part I). Thanks to

Vivek Wadwha for traveling with me to Delhi and Jaipur and for arguing with me most of the time, and thanks to NIIT and the TiE Network for your hospitality and introductions as well. A huge thanks to VSS Mani for introducing me to my first Bollywood star, and to Beerud Sheth for lending us Lenny when we needed him most. I can't thank the staff of VNL and Ravi Ghate enough for my time spent in a half-dozen Indian villages. Those were some of the best days of my entire reporting journey, and they will stay with me forever.

In Brazil, the biggest thank you has to go to Endeavor, whose network of entrepreneurs is unparalleled, especially Linda Rottenberg and Allen Taylor, who has the patience of a saint. Thanks also to Diego Simon, Giberto Alves, Julio Vasconcellos, Francisco Jardim, and Eric Acher. Thanks to Wences Casares for giving me your car when I was stranded. Huge thanks to Sidnei Borges dos Santos and the BS Construtora team for an amazing trip to the Amazon basin, to Marco Gomes for showing me his hometown, and to Alexadre Ribenboim and CDI for showing me a Rio *favela*—all indescribable experiences I hope I've done some justice to here.

Thanks to Bo Fishback of the Kauffman Foundation, who first told me I should go to Indonesia, and for all the support from Ciputra's organization in planning my trip, especially Agung Waluyo and Antonius Tanan. Huge thanks to Mr. Ciputra and Martha Tilaar for sharing your inspiring stories, and to Dino Patti Djalal the staff of Universitas Ciputra, and Rama Mamuaya and all of the budding Indonesian Web crew.

I want to thank everyone involved with the most moving of my travels, my two trips to Rwanda. Thanks to Dan Nova for a chance phone conversation in which you told me of your experiences and let me come with you on your next trip. Thanks to Paul Farmer and everyone at Partners in Health—you guys made me rethink the nature of global poverty and what the world should be doing about it. If this book makes any money, you are getting a nice donation. Thanks to Jean de Dieu Kagabo for sharing your amazing, inspirational story and for taking me out for a night on the town. Thanks to Adam, my driver, for showing me the country through your eyes. And thanks to all the Rwandans who wake up every day and work to build a better country, proving most of our Western preconceived notions wrong. And thanks to Alec Ross, Suzanne Hall, and the State Department for taking me along to Colombia. It was an unforgettable trip.

Lastly, a huge thanks to my parents in Memphis who've been inspirations my entire life, my in-laws who are even my fans when I fail, and all my close friends in San Francisco who supported me during a long, exhausting journey filled with ear infections, parasites, baboon attacks, and malaria scares. This was not an easy book to write, made harder because no one wanted me to write it. I couldn't have done it without Olivia Hine, Paul Carr, and of course my husband Geoffrey Ellis, who made more sacrifices for this project than anyone and supported me even as I plundered our life savings to report this book.

This book belongs to all of you.

1

Nothing to Lose

When Marco Gomes was five years old, his parents sent him to school in Brasilia, about 40 kilometers away from home. He'd ride the bus to town with his father, who had a job building sofas for the rich people who lived across the lake. Gomes' mother had already taught him to read, but she didn't know math, and she wanted him to learn it from the best public school she could send him to. That couldn't be found in his home village of Gama, and math would wind up being important for Gomes.

School let out before his father would get done with work. So five-year-old Gomes would walk a kilometer to the huge bus station in the middle of the 1960s-modernist architecture of Brazil's capital city. Every day, his mother drilled his name and address into his head until he could recite it on command, but he could only do it if he recited the entire thing:

Marco Gomes
Quadra 34, Numero 130,
Setor Leste,
Gama, DF,
Brasil

He'd mutter it over and over to himself so he wouldn't forget. Remembering that address was his only thread home. "I was like a robot," he says, driving around Brasilia today in his old Fiat. "Trained like a dog."

One afternoon, Gomes fell asleep on the bus and missed his stop. He found a policeman, walked up to him, tugged on his sleeve, and demanded: "Take me to your general." The amused cop took the gangly five-year-old to the station, where Gomes informed the captain he'd missed his stop and recited his address. The captain gave him a ride home in the front cabin of a paddy wagon normally reserved for hardened drug runners and smugglers—the ones Gomes knew in his neighborhood and his extended family. The paddy wagon pulled into Gama, sirens blaring, and his frightened neighbors poured out of their homes to see what the trouble was. Five-year-old Gomes bounded out with his backpack, saying "It's just me, everyone!"

Lesson 1: No matter what happens, I can make it on my own.

Gomes stopped going to school in Brasilia at six years old. His family could no longer afford the cost of his taking the bus and buying lunch every day. He missed the teachers. In Gama, many kids couldn't read until their teens or later, and he was bored sitting in class with them. He missed chasing the pigeons in Three Powers Square once class had ended, his arms and legs flailing. He even missed the bus.

Six-year-old Gomes came home to his parents' wooden shack, one of many homes he shuttled between in his early life. His father was hunched over a plate in the middle of the room. "Marco! Get in your room!" his mother shouted at him. His eyes stung with tears. He didn't like being in trouble, and he didn't know what he'd done.

He would later realize that plate was filled with cocaine, and his dad was an addict. That white powder his mother had always shielded him from was the biggest reason his parents didn't have money for him to take the bus anymore. It was the reason his parents fought. It was the reason his father lost a string of jobs. In years to come, the men who peddled that drug would gun down Gomes' cousin. The level of lethal violence in Brazil's slums, or *favelas,* is comparable to that of a modern civil war zone. In the worst areas, one in every five people has lost a loved one, many blaming the police for an inability or unwillingness to control the situation.[1] Gomes lost only a handful of close friends growing up, but talking about death in Gama was as routine as talking about the weather.

"You remember that guy who stood on that corner all the time?"

"Did you hear what happened to that kid with the white bike?"

Lesson 2: The quick money of Brazil's drug trade wasn't as glamorous as it looked.

When Gomes was eight years old, a friend took him to an evangelical Christian church. Brazil is the world's largest Catholic country, but in the late 1990s, evangelical Protestantism took root in the country's poorest communities, where the Catholic veil-of-tears worldview was offering little hope. From 1991 to 2000, Catholicism fell by 10 percent in Brazil, and Protestantism increased from 9 percent to 15 percent of the population, according to the national census.

In places like Gama, the movement doesn't operate in opulent churches; it spreads out through holed-out rooms in concrete strip malls, next to convenience stores or barbershops. There's never a cross, because that's too Catholic. Instead, you can spot an evangelical church by the rows of neat, white plastic chairs and the drum set.

Gomes fell in love with evangelical Christianity. He liked the stories, the songs, the feeling of community, the belief that there was something greater—someone up there watching and taking care of him. In a world where his peers were getting seduced by the quick money of the drug trade, Gomes found Jesus intoxicating.

He went home after church one night, and his parents were screaming at each other. They were on the verge of divorce. That night he began to convert them to Christianity. Over time he convinced his father to give up cocaine, and saved his parents' marriage. His dad has been clean ever since, and his parents are now evangelical ministers in Gama. "Outside it was still chaos, but at least inside the house it was better," he says.

Gomes can't explain what he said to his parents that night that was so powerful. "You can look at it from a psychological point of view and say that drugs had cost my father everything, and he was now about to lose his family, too," Gomes says a dozen years later. "Or you can look at it from the supernatural point of view and say God saved him. I don't care. He stopped doing drugs."

Lesson 3: No one was beyond redemption.

Gomes started building computers at 12 years old. His uncles were smugglers, buying toys in Paraguay and spiriting them across the Brazilian border, where they'd sell them on the black market. When his uncles got busted, they switched to smuggling computer parts; most of the parts were small, and they could reassemble them back in Brazil. Gomes loved to tiptoe around the parts while his uncles slept, teaching himself how to put the building blocks for opportunity and information together in the form of circuits, motherboards, and hard drives, like an elf repairing shoes while the cobblers slept in the next room.

A few years later, one of his uncles found himself racing through the jungle with six huge cathode-ray-tube monitors strapped around his torso, when he decided he needed to make a change.

After another bust, he went legit, opening a computer shop in a basement in north Brasilia, next to a sweat-soaked martial arts gym. He still assembled computers cheaply, but now he bought the parts in bulk through proper channels.

Gomes worked there every summer. He was yelled at when he made a mistake and teased ruthlessly in the way young boys are in a sprawling male-dominated family. But he made enough money to buy comic books and a skateboard, and he loved it.

His uncle's business—based entirely on word-of-mouth referrals—boomed. He was the richest person in Gomes' family. He had several houses, a car, and a speedboat that would cruise through Brasilia's crystal-clear, man-made Lake Paranoa, constructed in part to separate the rich government men from the poor. A single bus took the poor who worked for the rich across the lake in the morning, and a single bus took them back at night. They knew not to miss that bus. There was no other way across unless you had a car, or you had a boat like Gomes' uncle. "It was like the ones in *Baywatch*," Gomes says, adding sheepishly, "but unfortunately, we didn't have the girls."

Lesson 4: Crime doesn't pay, but computers do.

At 12 years old, Gomes got his first slow, dial-up Internet connection. He was as swept away as he'd been that first day in church. This connection introduced him to companies like Yahoo! and Google, and he read about the rich, powerful U.S. entrepreneurs behind these companies. He started teaching himself to code, not because he thought he'd be one of these entrepreneurs, but because he loved it the way he loved comic books and skateboards. The idea that he could build an Internet company was as ridiculous as the idea that he could become the next James Cameron just because he loved the *Terminator* movies. The thought didn't even occur to him.

It was like the days back when his father still had his sofa business, and Gomes would go on deliveries with him to the multi-million-dollar homes across the lake. Growing up in a world where degrees of poverty were measured by what the walls of your house were made from, Gomes gawked at the opulence. He saw a television set as tall as he was and stared at the ants in the Coca-Cola commercial that was playing at the time. On his tiny set at home, he could barely tell what the ants were, but on this set they were huge, vibrant, and pulsating with life. He could barely take his eyes off the TV, but it wasn't because he wanted it. This reality was too far from his life for Gomes to feel anything like envy. Like starting an Internet company, this TV was for other people, not for poor, half-educated Marco Gomes.

That was Lesson 5, only this time the lesson was wrong.

Ten years since he got that Internet connection, Gomes has founded his own Internet startup, taken venture funding, moved to São Paulo, and become an icon to other would-be Web entrepreneurs countrywide. In spring 2010, Gomes was on a flight to Europe, where he planned to propose to his girlfriend in Paris, France, and then pick up an entrepreneur award in Barcelona, Spain. His hands were sweating thinking of both events, and he couldn't help but reflect on his dramatic change in fortune.

Gomes had a lot of people to thank for how differently his life had turned out from the way it started: his mom for her determination that he study, his dad for getting clean, his uncle who taught him entrepreneurship wasn't just for drug runners, that friend who took him to church, and of course, the people who started the Internet. But mostly, Gomes had the 21st century to thank. Simply because of *when* he was born, *where* he was born didn't matter.

∞

This book is about great entrepreneurs—the brilliant, the crazy, the cocky, the driven—the people who create companies that change lives and do more to lift thousands out of poverty than most government programs or nongovernmental organizations. We're not talking about subsistence-level entrepreneurs operating off microloans. This book is about the kind of high-growth entrepreneurs who are the dreamers, visionaries, megalomaniacs, and arrogant sons-of-bitches who see the world in a different way and set out to build businesses for reasons they can't always articulate; they just can't do otherwise. It's the kind of entrepreneurship that's created companies like FedEx, Apple, Google, and Microsoft and inspired millions more that they could do the same. And now, it's remaking the world.

Throughout corners of Asia, Eastern Europe, Africa, the Middle East, and Latin America, a combination of historical, geopolitical, technological, financial, social, and macroeconomic forces have created a primordial soup from which a new powerful generation of entrepreneurs are emerging. The West has two choices: Invest and partner with them or get shoved out of the way.

The world tends to think of Silicon Valley when it thinks of this type of entrepreneurship, but that's going to change in the next few decades, and the flow of money and talent is going to change with it. The point of this book isn't to discover the next Silicon Valley. There is no single next Silicon Valley. Communications and globalization has created a new world where the next great companies can come from anywhere, especially as a multibillion-person-strong, consuming middle class is rising, spread across geographies that were considered economic wastelands for much of the 20th century.

Because of the growth of Western multinationals in the developing world and the general meshing of cultures in the modern Internet age, this new entrepreneur is unlike what the world has seen before. This new entrepreneur is a mishmash between the mom-and-pop traders and retailers associated with the old world, contented to make enough to feed his or her family and little else, and the modern venture-funded, all-about-growth entrepreneurs of Silicon Valley.

These entrepreneurs live in a shrunken, globalized world. They may be grappling with emerging market problems, but their role models aren't someone in a nearby village. They are frequently names like Bill Gates, Steve Jobs, or even Donald Trump and Walt

Disney. These entrepreneurs have an inkling of how modern venture capital works. They know tiny companies can become huge powerhouses quickly. They know high risk can be highly rewarded. They know David can beat Goliath. And this new global entrepreneur has three big advantages.

The first one is the home field advantage. Americans may wish the next few decades' growth was in the American heartland where the demise of manufacturing has left millions unemployed and local economies sputtering, but it's not. It's in emerging markets. Goldman Sachs first argued this point to Wall Street in 2001 with a paper entitled "Building Better Global Economic BRICs,"[2] in which the investment bank predicted that Brazil, Russia, India, and China would make up more than 10 percent of the world GDP by 2010. By 2007, it was already 15 percent. So much for the all-important G7 nations of Canada, France, Germany, Italy, Japan, the United Kingdom, and the United States; by the middle of this century, the seven largest economies in the world will be China, the United States, India, Brazil, Mexico, Russia, and Indonesia.[3]

In these countries, growing middle classes are driving that growth, not simply the luxury purchases of the wealthy or corporate and government spending. Established U.S. companies with billions in resources would love nothing more than to pilfer those billions of new consumers for themselves. The problem is that they're not always good at it. For example, KFC may have dominated China's fast-food scene, but none of the Valley's Internet companies have done well there. The reality is that no place knows a big local market better than local entrepreneurs.

The second advantage is that in today's globalized world, money and talent don't have boundaries; they flow where the opportunity is. And the flow has already started to the emerging world. Right now, there is more than $100 billion in venture capital and private equity hungry to make money off the developing world, especially after the zero stock market growth over the last decade in the United States.

Meanwhile, many of the immigrants who came to the United States over the last few decades seeking opportunity are returning home. Duke Researcher Vivek Wadhwa expects hundreds of thousands of immigrants will return home to China and India in the next five years. Many more are getting shoved out of the United States by an increasingly hostile attitude toward immigrants and H-1b Visa holders. Still more who might have come to the United States a few years ago for college or graduate school aren't coming now. The year 2009 was the first year that foreign-born admissions to top U.S. grad schools *fell*.

It's almost impossible to know what the opportunity cost would be if substantially fewer immigrants come to the United States, but it's a clear disadvantage when it comes to entrepreneurship. One-quarter of successful Silicon Valley companies were started by immigrants. If the United States hadn't been the land of opportunity, we wouldn't have Intel, PayPal, Google, Yahoo!, or a host of other industry giants, and that doesn't include the thousands of immigrants who fuel the management ranks and research-and-development (R&D) corps throughout the technology industry.

The final advantage is the hardest to quantify: These emerging markets and their entrepreneurs have nothing to lose. When a country, industry, or entrepreneur has nothing to lose, it is freed from all the normal restrictions of the way things are usually done. Having nothing to lose gives one the luxury of starting with a clean sheet of paper and far more freedom to take risk—or, as it's called in business circles, a *greenfield opportunity*. It's the reason South Korea has better broadband than the United States ever will. It's the reason I can get a clear cell phone signal amid pygmy huts in central Africa but not in my living room in San Francisco. It's the reason Japanese cities are connected by futuristic bullet trains that New York and Los Angeles may never have.

Look at entrepreneurs in the United States: Overwhelmingly, the most successful ones came from the most modest backgrounds: the immigrant who came to the United States with nothing, the kid whose family couldn't afford a college education, the awkward D-student that no one believed in, and the most iconic Valley trope, the dropout. The more disenfranchised a person is, the more incentive he or she has to upend the established order. The American dream is the very idea that having nothing allows you to take enough risk that you can achieve anything.

There's paradoxical fickleness to the advantage of having nothing to lose, however. By its very nature, it doesn't last forever. And for those who realize they've lost it, it's impossible to get back.

∞

This is not another book about globalization. You won't find accounts of whole middle classes being formed thanks to Western factories, research labs, and call centers. In the countries this book will take you to, we'll sidestep the gleaming office parks bearing well-known names like Google, Microsoft, and Oracle. Neither is this a book about how U.S. businesspeople can simply profit off of increasingly well-educated, hard-working, cheaper employees in developing nations.

That is where the story of this new wave of entrepreneurship begins. Just as the old imperialist empires sought to keep growing by annexing new territories rich with natural resources, so too have Western multinationals sought to use the emerging world to keep top lines growing, bottom lines shrinking, and stock prices soaring. The rise of global entrepreneurship has as much to do with the decline of growth in the United States as it has to do with the increase of opportunities in the developing world.

Let's examine the United States first. At some point in the last decade, the United States just stopped growing. From 2000 to 2010, very few jobs were created, and it was the first decade on record where the number of private-sector jobs actually *shrank*. The typical family got no economic boost at all from 2000 to 2010. There was no appreciation in home prices and zero gains in stocks, when averaged across all Americans.[4]

Of course, this zero growth is an average. In Silicon Valley, plenty of new millionaires and billionaires were minted from 2000 to 2010, and many more will continue to be minted in the future. The point isn't that no one in the United States made money, it's that those wins were the exceptions, and they came at the expense of so many others losing money that overall the United States flat-lined as a nation.

Perhaps the American dream just worked too well. Old industries like steel, railroads, and utilities had long ago run their course in the United States. So too had the buildout of department stores, malls, sprawling fast-food chains, and big-box retailers. Media—whether radio, TV, movies, or news—was also largely saturated. And most of the old, once-proud industries like automobile manufacturing hadn't innovated and kept up with what customers wanted and the environment needed.

This slowdown would have hit the United States far harder, far sooner if it weren't for the information technology revolution. A PC in every household and cubicle is an awful lot of PCs. Hello, new growth industry! And PCs on every desk lead to networks. That led to a multibillion-dollar wave of spending on corporate software that would mint dozens of new billion-dollar companies in a matter of years. On top of this, the unleashing of the Internet was a seminal moment for modern entrepreneurship. Growth in telecom, enterprise software, consumer software, laptops, and smartphones exploded. Meanwhile, the Internet injected new growth into many of the United States' most stagnated industries, such as retail, media, and travel.

The carnage from the March 2000 dot-com crash aside, a lot of real value was created during the 1990s, but the 2000s would be a different matter. In many ways, the economic recovery in the early 2000s did more damage than good. In the consumer sphere, growth was fueled by a housing boom and credit card debt. According to the St. Louis branch of the Federal Reserve Bank, household debt more than doubled from 2000 to 2010, rising from just above $6 billion to peak at nearly $14 billion.

In the corporate sphere, the post-2000 recovery was largely a jobless one lead by huge gains in productivity. With rare exceptions like Google, Silicon Valley's great public company–generating machine all but ground to a halt, and the United States went through a sizable shift in its collective corporate culture, where layoffs were no longer a move of last resort for a dying company but a regular way to meet earnings estimates for even highly profitable companies.

Meanwhile, workers' output was continually squeezed, without much wage appreciation. From 2000 to 2005, the median hourly pay adjusted for inflation declined, according to the Economic Policy Institute, as worker productivity rose, according to the Bureau of Labor Statistics. By 2006, wages were at their lowest share of gross domestic product on record, whereas corporate profits were at their highest share in nearly 50 years, according to the Department of Commerce.

There are only so many hours you can pry out of U.S. workers, however, and there is only so little you can pay them. That's where outsourcing and the emerging world came in. It seemed too good to be true: high-quality workers who were happy to work long hours for a fraction of the cost. And thanks to that vast buildout of communications, computers, and the Internet, people argued that a globally flung, outsourced company could function as one tight organization.

The United States was lauded as something even greater than a place that could make things. It was becoming a so-called knowledge economy. The United States was the place that would dream up the big ideas, like iPods, smartphones, and eBook readers, and send them off for someone else to actually build.

Business professors like David B. Yoffie of Harvard Business School argued that we weren't outsourcing anything of value, as the United States was becoming more of a high-margin service economy. The high-value intellectual work—whether design, strategy, or engineering—was all still being done in the United States. If you could get the low-value work done elsewhere at a fraction of the price, how was that a bad thing? Some pundits argued that these companies were helping humanity by giving poor people in the emerging world comfortable, comparatively high-paying jobs.

It was a flattened, globalized world, and this was the United States's new role in it. It was a modern imperial superpower for a new age. It was oh-so-benevolently allowing the rest of the world to do the work Americans didn't want to do, paying them more than they could make otherwise, teaching them valuable professional skills. And yet at the same time, U.S. companies could make more money, earn bigger profits, and have higher stock prices—a win-win situation. There would be one virtual workforce coursing throughout the globe, impervious to borders, like blood coursing through a body. Each organ would do what it was uniquely good at, and that blood would all flow back to the central control spot—the heart. Or, in the case of globalization—the United States.

Of course, like most things taught at business school, parts of this ideology are true, and parts only look good on paper. "The prevailing view of the past 25 years has been that the U.S. can thrive as a center of innovation and leave the manufacturing of products it invents and designs to others," wrote Gary P. Pisano of Harvard Business School. "Nothing could be further from the truth."[5] There were two big gaps in reasoning. The first is that manufacturing couldn't be cleanly divorced from invention—it's the cycle of making things that spawns new ideas for how things can be made better. By not making anything anymore, the United States is losing touch with how to invent.

The second problem was that the emerging world wasn't just full of people who were only good at answering phones or low-level assembly, any more than all Americans were good at being big-idea visionaries like Steve Jobs. Pisano writes, "All this assumes your manufacturing partner is content to subsist on your table scraps. But what if they have their eye on the prime rib, too? Well, once they have learned to manufacture your product (and your ability to manufacture has eroded), they are in a much better position to move up the food chain into manufacturing and designing more sophisticated components and subsystems and, eventually, the entire product."[6]

Put more crassly—the world wasn't full of grunts who would be forever grateful for the United States's grunt work. The idea that China, India, and other areas of Southeast Asia would blithely recognize the United States's right to dominate intelligent, highly valued labor was at best naïve and at worst racist. Ironically, in trying to use the rest of the world's natural resources to grow, the United States jumpstarted that new entrepreneur class and the ecosystem it needs to grow without us—whether that's local management talent, trained coders, newly wealthy local angel investors, or just the Western capitalist mentality.

The concept of the American dream may be our biggest cultural export—bigger than Coca-Cola, Coach, and KFC put together. The same communications tools that allowed a factory in China to be connected to, say, Apple executives in Cupertino, California, also showed this global emerging middle class the lifestyle of the West and the marvels of high-growth modern entrepreneurship.

Imagine you were a coder working for Amazon in India. The day you got the job, you couldn't believe your luck. They were going to pay you $12,000 a year to code in a comfortable office, and that's far more than your parents ever made. To your family, it was greater prestige than becoming a doctor. Indian coders like these developed some of the most sophisticated circuitry that went into Amazon's eBook reader, the Kindle. That's a huge cost savings for Amazon and a job for the coder that's much higher up the design chain than basic factory assembly. But very little of the *value* of that work actually stayed in India; the bulk of it flowed right back to Amazon's coffers in Seattle, Washington. India got a few well-paying jobs, and that was pretty much it.

Just like that coder, India as a country was initially thrilled for all these high-dollar R&D jobs, and even now it's difficult to find anyone who would argue that the sprawling high-tech office complexes of Bangalore haven't been a tremendous boon for the country for the most part. But toward the end of the 2000s, the country and its most prominent businesspeople started to realize there was only one way to retain the value of their natural resources of labor and intelligence: local entrepreneurship.

One hundred years from now, when we look back on the 21st century, the dominant story won't be one of the emerging world graciously serving as the West's inexhaustible source of low-cost labor and growing middle classes hungry for new goods and services. It'll be the story of the formation of new, raw superpowers violently and chaotically bursting through the world's floorboards. And it won't be the story of politicians. It'll be the story of entrepreneurs like Marco Gomes.

Just as the exploration and colonization of the Americas set the stage for the rise of the United States and its 50-plus-year reign as the world's greatest superpower, so too is the exploration and exploitation of the emerging world's business resources leading to something new, exciting, and hugely powerful: an unprecedented tsunami of economic growth that will change the world's political and business landscape forever. While many entrepreneurial ventures will fail spectacularly—undoubtedly a higher percentage than those that will fail in the United States—there will be far larger overall growth.

When it comes to sectors, the opportunities are as varied as the challenges these countries face. Rapid industrialization and urbanization have spurred the need for a new, more modern infrastructure. New access to television and the Internet has meant that local media and entertainment are developing for the first time, and with it modern-day versions of Madison Avenue, Hollywood, and San Francisco all crammed together. Everything from basic manufacturing to consumer services as varied as driving schools or new fast-food chains are being built out for the first time, too.

In most developing countries, mobile telephony is a hothouse of innovation. Billions of people in the poorest villages may not have electricity or running water, but they have mobile phones, and those phones are changing their lives. That's lead to a flurry of new services that couldn't be delivered before, such as banking, education, ecommerce, and even games. It's as if the industries that took decades to develop in the West are all growing at once in the emerging world, and not just in one country but across China, India, Latin America, Africa, Southeast Asia, and Eastern Europe.

But that very lack of basic infrastructure—and in many cases functioning governments—creates as much havoc as it does opportunity. Emerging markets are not for those with a weak stomach. Life and investing there is difficult. There's a cultural, business, and ethical quandary around every corner. As many of the Western world's businesses and investors have already realized, however, the promise is just too big to ignore, especially given the flattening growth in the West.

These new world entrepreneurs have friends in high places. In China, Jack Ma, CEO of ecommerce giant Alibaba Group, gives keynotes, mentors young entrepreneurs, and even starred in an *Apprentice*-style show to encourage more entrepreneurship in the country. In India, N. R. Narayana Murthy, founder of outsourcing juggernaut Infosys, sold 800,000 shares of his company to start investing in young, local entrepreneurs. In sub-Saharan Africa, eBay founder Pierre Omidyar launched a fund to make Western-style equity investments in startups, determined to give away some 90 percent of his eBay billions to make the world a more equitable place. In Latin America, Endeavor, a nonprofit organization, has mentored and helped raise funding for more than 400 entrepreneurs who generate a combined $3.15 billion in annual revenues and have created more than 98,000 high-paying jobs. In Indonesia, 80-year-old real estate billionaire Ir. Ciputra has made it his mission to educate and mentor millions of local high-growth entrepreneurs. In Rwanda, President Paul Kagame courts investments from U.S. venture capitalists and businesspeople, and in Haiti, former President Bill Clinton has championed not donations, but equity-based venture capital as a way of finally pulling the beleaguered nation out of poverty.

These leaders aren't talking about feel-good social entrepreneurship. The idea is that real, greed-based startup investing is the best, sustainable way to dramatically improve poverty, quality of life, modernization, and even peace throughout the developing world. Investing in local entrepreneurship is not only the new handout; it's the new way out.

∝⧖⧖∝

This promise of entrepreneurship in emerging markets is about more than the Wall Street–oriented BRIC ideology. Things like large bond issues to construct a mega-nation's infrastructure or a deal to privatize huge government-owned utilities are clear-cut opportunities that can be analyzed with a spreadsheet, but the world of high-growth entrepreneurship cannot.

Entrepreneurship is an inherently individualistic, cultural, and a frequently irrational phenomenon. If computers and math could predict innovation, Silicon Valley wouldn't be a unique phenomenon in the world. If it were that easy, we'd all be billionaires. The Valley is littered with companies that should have made it based on market opportunity, team, and timing, but for inexplicable reasons didn't. So, too, will the opportunities in the emerging world be uneven and unpredictable.

Similarly, emerging markets aren't emerging together in one monolith. Rather, they're emerging chaotically, in fits and starts and in distinct waves. Consider India and China: Early in the last decade, venture capital and private equity shops saw two huge countries with 1 billion people each that modernization had largely bypassed, and they saw huge opportunity.

Many prized India over China, given India's similarities to the West in language and politics. Those investors were wrong. China leapfrogged ahead of India in most industries, not to mention social change and infrastructure. But that doesn't make India any less of an opportunity—it's just on a different trajectory. In China, entrepreneurs have to build a company that can move incredibly fast, whereas in India, entrepreneurs have to build a company that can survive as a market moves incredibly slowly. A one-size-fits-all investment approach won't work.

Nuances like these are part of what makes the trend more difficult to invest in but far more lucrative long-term. We're not dealing with one country showing growth anymore than we're dealing with one industry showing growth. Emerging markets can't be called a bubble. At worst, the trend represents many bubbles, and each of them popping at the same time is unlikely. In addition, these countries are all investing in and selling to one another. That means the money created in a country that's surging is frequently flowing back into the entire emerging-market ecosystem. And in many cases, an unaware United States is being left out.

Rather than just picking the four obvious BRIC countries, I wanted to give readers a more nuanced analysis of new world entrepreneurship, what's happening on the ground now, what it looks and feels like, where it's going, and where it's needed. Many of the reasons for selecting these countries can't be summed up in a spreadsheet. It's the result of the entrepreneurial stories and environments I found there. If the rise of Silicon Valley—once a sleepy 50-mile stretch of fruit orchards—has taught us anything, it's that the best string of returns don't always come from the places we expect.

A country even more emblematic of that unpredictability is Israel. Entrepreneurship expanded dramatically in Israel in the 1990s. Per capita, this tiny nation with few inherent advantages received twice as much venture capital as the United States and a whopping 30 times more than Europe. Israel is home to more NASDAQ traded companies than any other non-U.S. country. Even before global venture capital investing became fashionable, billions flowed into Israel for one main reason: Israelis made great entrepreneurs. To them, quitting your job to start a new company wasn't particularly risky. Israelis quite literally live like there is no tomorrow, because that's how you survive on a sandy strip the size of New Jersey that's surrounded by enemies.

From there we go to China, a nation that is difficult to call emerging anymore. China is the largest, most modern, and wealthiest of all of these countries, and hence, it is the model even with its flaws. Right now, there's fear that China is a bubble waiting to pop, engorged by constant government spending and runaway housing prices. That may be the case, but even if it happens, China's run won't be over. The country has nearly $3 trillion in cash reserves and an urban infrastructure that's the envy of even the developed world. Then there's the simple math: When you multiply 1.3 billion by any number, the result is big.

We'll then turn to India and Brazil, two nations struggling to maintain their growth and meet their burgeoning populations' social needs with semi-dysfunctional, young democracies. Although both have issues with corruption and poverty, little else in these countries is the same.

Then we'll take an unconventional turn toward more nascent emerging markets in Southeast Asia and Africa. We'll look at these economies through the examples of Indonesia, the world's largest Muslim country with 240 million residents, and Rwanda, the tiniest, most densely populated, poorest, and yet—for many investors—one of the most promising African countries right now.

But first let's start with the United States's own engine for growth, Silicon Valley. Understanding what the Valley has done well is crucial to understanding what these corners of the emerging world are seeking to build. We'll examine what emerging markets have gleaned from the Valley, why this growth engine has stagnated in the last decade, and what role the Valley elite hopes to play in this new global entrepreneurship drama.

2

The Death of Risk in America

*I*t is February 2009, and I am sitting on the patio of a coffee shop upstairs in a mall. The scene would be totally unremarkable except that this mall is in Kigali, Rwanda, and I'm talking about the economics of toilet paper.

It's hard not to gaze out at the vista of Rwanda's famous rolling hills. Half of them are swarmed with *favela*-like shanty buildings, and the rest are dotted with modern stucco mansions under construction. Kigali is a city in stunningly rapid transition.

Along the sides of the freshly paved streets winding up to this mall are workers in prison jumpsuits digging ditches—a sight that's only ominous when my guide tells me they're imprisoned murderers from the bloody 1994 Rwandan genocide out on a work-release program. It's important to Rwanda's President Paul Kagame that everyone in the country literally and figuratively helps rebuild the war-torn country. *Everyone.* "Hutu" and "Tutsi" are taboo words these days. "We are all Rwandans" is the country's modern-day mantra. Seeing them holding shovels and other crude, blunt instruments that were not too long ago used to bash in Tutsi skulls is chilling, but I seem to be the only one bothered by it.

Sitting with me is Jean de Dieu Kagabo. He's 28 years old. He lost his parents in the genocide and its aftermath, along with nearly 1 million of his fellow Rwandans. He saw things no one should see. And now, some 15 years later, he's a Central African consumer package goods mogul with several German luxury cars and a summer house on the lake next to President Kagame's.

Talking to Kagabo is as disorienting as looking at those hills that simultaneously show glimpses of Rwanda's past and Rwanda's future. Things are moving so quickly in Rwanda, that it's almost as if there's no such thing as Rwanda's present. Kagabo has what I can only call "Rwandan eyes." There's an otherworldly stillness and depth to them that I'd never seen before, but I see it all across this country—even in the eyes of children. They're eyes that have seen more evil than most of us ever will. Even when Kagabo is laughing, his eyes are not.

We're not talking about these things though. We're talking about toilet paper. Having spent the previous decade of my career parsing business pitches on medical devices, new drug compounds, chipsets, rational databases, super routers, and Web sites, I can't remember the last time I had this un-techy of a conversation.

But here's the remarkable part: Just as those McMansions on the hills could be under construction anywhere in the world, as I sit and talk business with Kagabo, I can't stop thinking about how much he reminds me of an entrepreneur I'd recently interviewed in the United States: Tony Hsieh, CEO of the ecommerce shoe company, Zappos.com. Part of this resemblance is physical: Both men have thin, slight builds, close-cropped hair, and boyish faces. Neither is particularly emotive or talkative. They both answer direct questions, succinctly and without pretense in a soft-spoken tone, more out of shyness than any sort of coldness.

There's also a similarity in what they say, or more to the point, in the way they think. Both men have a knack for looking at a problem and finding a common-sense solution. They are able to tune out every best-practice piece of advice a consultant would give them or every reason a more mature CEO would tell them their idea wouldn't work. Almost like the kid in the story "The Emperor Has No Clothes," for both Kagabo and Hsieh, the obvious answer is the right one, and no one will persuade them otherwise.

Zappos, for instance, was a dot-com survivor that shouldn't have survived. When faced with the concern that shoes were too difficult to purchase online because fit matters and can vary so wildly across brands, Hsieh solved this problem with a common-sense solution. Zappos would pay for the shipping and returns so people could order several different sizes, styles, or colors and just send the rest back. He'd even pay to have a UPS driver come to your house to pick the boxes up. He also gave every customer a surprise upgrade to priority shipping. The hidden truth behind Zappos' nearly $1 billion in gross merchandise sales in 2009 was the fact that some 40 percent were returns—and Hsieh was fine with that.

Of course, some competitors argued that Zappos had killed their business models by setting such expensive customer expectations, but Hsieh's approach solved the customer loyalty problem. That was more important to Hsieh, because Zappos wasn't just selling shoes, it was selling "happiness," in his words.

It was a way of constructing a business that no seasoned manager would have ever allowed, but Hsieh saw this clearly and believed that it was the only way to build a billion-dollar ecommerce business for long-term success. He wasn't going to stop at shoes either. Zappos started selling cookware because customers suggested it, and he stated that he could see a scenario where one day Zappos might have its own airline. A decade later, Amazon.com paid $1.2 billion for the company—not because of its margins on shoes, but because of what it meant in consumers' minds and hearts. Hsieh was right.

Kagabo takes a similar, almost childlike approach to his business. He started manufacturing toilet paper when he was 18 because he needed money to feed his family, no one made it locally, and—in good times and bad—everyone needs it. As we sat on this patio, he was telling me about his company, Soft Group's, plans to get into bottled water—a market that's considerably more crowded, with several government-sponsored bottling plants.

His way into this market wasn't by offering better water or cheaper prices. Like Hsieh, it was by solving an important customer problem. Although there's no armed robbery in Rwanda, there is petty theft, and local merchants were seeing pallets of water disappear, leading them to believe employees were pilfering them. These mom-and-pop shops couldn't afford pricey surveillance systems, so the water costs were escalating. Enter Kagabo's commonsense solution: He'd give each store bottles of water with their own labels on them. Consider it a low-tech version of a LoJack®: If the merchants see pallets of water for resale at market days with their brand on it, they can easily figure out where their missing pallets of water went. The thieves were likely to be caught, so petty theft at these stores would decrease.

"Entrepreneur" is a fashionable mantle nearly everyone wraps themselves in these days, but this is what a conversation with a great entrepreneur is like. It's not about technology or features or acronyms—it's a way of thinking and problem solving, coupled with the internal compass to believe in the idea and the confidence and determination to carry it out.

Great entrepreneurs' minds just work differently than other people's. They can see solutions to problems clearly. And while those solutions seem to make obvious sense when explained, few others would have come up with them. You can't describe great entrepreneurs by the kind of companies they are starting, their ages, their backgrounds, or their ethnicity—it's by the way their minds works.

True entrepreneurship can't be taught. It can't be faked. It can't be silenced. You either have it or you don't. And just because we hear the most about U.S. entrepreneurs, that doesn't mean we have a lock on it. Increasingly, even Silicon Valley—the hub of U.S. entrepreneurship—is losing stories like Hsieh and, with it, what made America and the Valley great.

⁓≫

In the 1800s, being an entrepreneur was associated with building something when you had nothing or simply with the luxury of working for yourself. It held the promise of building a nice, profitable business you could pass on to your kids. Every once in a while, a company would come out of it, but that wasn't really the end goal of the early days of U.S. entrepreneurship. There was a focus on lifestyle: making enough income so your children could have more than you did and building something you could own and be proud of. There was no glamour to it, and even if you succeeded, in many parts of the United States you were relegated to disdainful new money status.

Over the 100 years after the first immigrants passed through Ellis Island, the concept of entrepreneurship in America would change pretty dramatically. In 1958, a new law concerning investments in small businesses allowed the formation of a new kind of investing called venture capital. It was pioneered by successful entrepreneurs and restless bankers who were seeking to fill a hole in our finance system—one that had huge risk but potentially lucrative rewards. At the time, public companies could always raise more money to invest in the growth of their business via a secondary stock offering or a bond issue. Private companies could get bank loans. Although some small businesses could get Small Business Administration

(SBA) loans, an entrepreneur who had a great idea but no collateral, no business plan, and, in some cases, no product had few options.

When they do their jobs right, venture capitalists take huge risks. They back someone unknown and an idea that seems crazy. In exchange for that risk, they get a huge chunk of ownership in the company, on average 20 percent per funding round. If the idea is good enough, entrepreneurs can use the investment to jumpstart the business, sidestepping the years of lean margins and hard work an old-world entrepreneur might have had to endure building a business out of its own cash flow. If a company can get to hyper-growth, using a combination of a smart entrepreneur's disruptive idea and millions in backing, there's the potential for huge returns for the venture capitalists (VCs) and the entrepreneur. To counter the inevitable—and desired—risk in the asset class, investors pick many bets and hope one turns out to be big enough to pay for the losses of the rest. In a weird way, investors want to see losses. Without them, they probably aren't taking enough risks.

Venture capital started in Boston, but the combination of that method of investing and the burgeoning high-tech industry really lead to venture capital's explosion. And Silicon Valley dominated technology and ushered in a remaking of what it meant to be an entrepreneur.

By the late 1990s, Silicon Valley was a well-oiled machine. There was fluid interaction between Stanford University, nearby Sand Hill Road where dozens of VC firms were located, and a burgeoning working class of techies who embraced the risk of leaving an established job to go work for a new hotshot with a great idea. People in the Valley bonded because they were all immigrants and outcasts, somewhere on the spectrum between visionary and delusional. For every early Valley entrepreneur, there was a wife or mother somewhere sobbing and pleading with them to come to their senses. But over several decades, people saw the model work, watched as everyday people become millionaires, and believed in a place where smarts were all that mattered—a place where anyone could be the next great robber baron.

Unlike in Boston, there was a sense of openness in Silicon Valley. Competitors were also friends. Employees freely jumped between companies, sharing knowledge and ideas. VCs and angels invested in multiple companies, and they helped build bridges between potential partners and even helped orchestrate acquisitions. Even when someone's company gets bought, the non-compete clauses only last a few years. Companies in the Valley want to stay on top because they're the best, not through contracts, intimidation, and legislation. After the March 2000 NASDAQ crash, no Valley companies were asking for bailouts.

Despite its core of invention, the Valley loathes patent lawsuits, because usually they're waged by a so-called patent troll squatting on an idea that he or she never worked to turn into a business. Great entrepreneurs know an idea is just that. It's the execution, the sleepless nights, the years living on the edge that create a billion-dollar business. And unlike more rigid East Coast societies, there was no stigma to new money. Rather, new money meant you'd *earned* your wealth, and that gained you not only respect but also fame and adoration.

Within the United States, a pilgrimage started to take place from the Midwest, the South, and even the former center of innovation and finance—the Northeast. Globally, it was more pronounced than ever. In the 1980s and 1990s, more than 50 percent of Silicon Valley startups had one or more immigrants as a key founder, according to Duke University researcher Vivek Wadhwa. For immigrants like Andy Grove of Intel, Vinod Khosla of Sun Microsystems, Max Levchin of PayPal, and Sergey Brin of Google, Silicon Valley was the epicenter of the American dream.

The Internet took the sleepy town and stealthy industry of Silicon Valley and turbocharged it, displaying it to the world. The Valley had long had a core of enthusiasm, hubris, creativity, and greed, but now it was everywhere you turned, from north of the Golden Gate Bridge to the ho-hum depths of the East Bay to the once-sleepy orchards of the South Bay, and even down to the hippy beaches of Santa Cruz. You didn't even have to be that smart to do well, whether you were building a business amid the expensive and technical rollout of fiber optics and data centers, or you were selling computers and routers to every household now that the Internet made computers cool, or you were building the wonky behind-the-scenes software like databases that ran the whole thing. The Internet was such a concentrated, yet ever-reaching land grab of opportunity that nearly every business decision seemed insane and yet insane-to-pass-up at the same time.

It was in the great 1990s Internet bubble that Silicon Valley— the entrepreneurs behind it and the investors who fed money into the system—became famous. The idea of entrepreneurship morphed into something glitzy and glamorous, associated more with greed and ambition than pride and a nice lifestyle. While the word *entrepreneurship* merely took on new connotations, the phrase *small business* wouldn't do; instead, the Valley coined the term *startup*. Inherent in the phrase *small business* is the idea that it won't grow; inherent in the term *startup* is the idea that it will grow fast, get bought, or die. Small businesses were what old-world entrepreneurs started; modern entrepreneurs created startups. Silicon Valley exalted and transformed what it meant to be an entrepreneur in the United States, in the way that Hollywood exalted and transformed what it meant to be an actor. Silicon Valley was the place where modern entrepreneurs made it.

Of course, there was a problem with this. All that money flowing around the Valley and all the opportunity essentially derisked an economy that got its start and thrived particularly because it was so risky. That meant as more money flowed into the venture capital system, returns got worse, which drove investors into the arms of emerging markets. But before we talk about that shift, let's look at why returns fell after the 2000-era boom.

Too Much Cash

Because venture capital was so little written about before the Internet boom, many people don't realize how inflated it became. In 1996 the industry was investing a collective $12 billion, and by 2000 that ballooned to $106 billion. Single firms were raising $1 billion or more at a time, more than double the average just a few years earlier. After the dot-com crash, many firms voluntarily lowered their fund sizes from $1 billion each to $400 million or so, but more money kept flowing into the industry. The assets of institutional investors like pension funds and endowments were swelling with appreciation in real estate and other assets, and many of them were upping the allocations for private equity. The crash notwithstanding, there was exponentially more demand to invest in venture capital firms than ever before.

Many in the industry warned against the ramifications of this approach. Influential firms like Sequoia Capital refused to raise more than they thought they could feasibly invest, leaving hundreds of millions on the table. In a 2003 keynote in San Francisco to other limited partners, Fred Giuffrida of fund-of-funds Horsley Bridge Partners delivered a fire-and-brimstone speech warning of the excess funds pouring into the industry. During a presentation, Giuffrida showed a slide depicting a huge elephant trying to fit into a tiny box. His point was that far too many limited partners were shoving an unsustainable amount of money into venture capital. This elephant represented $1 trillion wedging its way into an asset class that had only returned $88 billion from 1990 to 1997. The math just didn't work, he argued, pleading with firms to lower their allocations, but few did.

Institutional investors were sick of Ivy League endowments like Yale and Harvard hogging all those fat venture returns and getting credit for being investing geniuses. Meanwhile, venture capitalists found it difficult to turn down money when they got a healthy

2 percent to 3 percent of assets under management to run the business. Whereas in earlier years that 2 percent to 3 percent was barely enough to pay rents and keep the lights on, in the post-1990s, the funds were so big that venture capitalists could live like kings whether they had a hit or not.

Everyone in the ecosystem knew the odds: 2 percent of startups funded since the 1980s made up some 98 percent of the returns, and only 5 percent of the VCs investing made more than 90 percent of those same returns. The institutions that invest in VCs just believed (or deluded themselves) that they were investing in that 2 percent to 10 percent that would win big. And if not? Well, it was still only 10 percent of their portfolios, at most.

This deluge of available money meant more than just a greater number of losses. It led to a systemic culture where no one had any skin in the game. VCs weren't dependent on returns to make millions, and when there was this much money looking to fund any good idea, there was no reason for entrepreneurs to invest their own money and no expectation for companies to bootstrap themselves the way they had in the past. Founders could easily get funding, get a nice salary, and in subsequent rounds cash out some of their equity far before there was an IPO or acquisition—something that was unheard of in the early days of venture capital.

To be fair, many entrepreneurs did bootstrap their companies anyway and would refuse large salaries. Unfortunately for investors, these were the better entrepreneurs. They were the ones who had made money already, and they knew the dangers of taking too much venture capital too soon. They wanted to retain control and wanted to make the biggest share of the returns when they hit it big. Because the cost of starting a Web or software company had plummeted some 90 percent since the late 1990s, it was a lot easier to bootstrap something than in the past. So in essence, there was adverse selection, and VCs got stakes in the worst startups, the unproven kids, and the entrepreneurs looking for a flip or quick money acquisition.

Similarly, there are a lot of reasons why it makes sense for a founder to take some capital off the table by cashing in shares. It makes the founder more likely to hold out for a big exit than to sell on the cheap early. But there's no doubt—it made being an entrepreneur more of a rational job than an unexplainable passion. It couldn't help but make the Valley more mercenary and more mainstream. The venture business became less about finding those elusive home runs and more about doing slightly better than break-even on each deal. It was an antirisk trap. With each big hit like YouTube that a VC firm missed, the more the partners had to play it safe, because they couldn't risk big losses.

This lack of having to make a big return to stay employed for founders and stay in business for VCs trickled down through the Valley ecosystem. Given that even profitable public technology companies were regularly laying off employees as a way to meet quarterly earnings, there was suddenly *less risk* in working at a startup than at the types of companies once considered stable and safe. Employees at startups got an equivalent salary, stock options that may or may not be worth something one day, and generally a more flexible work environment.

But this was the curse of the Valley's great company-formation, money-making machine becoming common knowledge. It was no longer just the believers and risk takers who played a part in it. In a bid to become the place where there was zero stigma against risk or failure, the Valley eradicated the things that are good about having a fear of failure. Namely, the rush, commitment, and passion that comes with having skin in the game.

End of a High-Tech Era

Part of all that me-too investing was the fault of limited partners who put way too much money in the hands of VCs, part of it was the fault of VCs, and part of it was just the by-product of a lull in the technology industry. The great Silicon Valley cycle that had begun with the semiconductor and rippled through computers and software and laptops and telecom to end with the Internet had just run its course. By 2006, excitement was building in the Valley again with a new lot of Web companies—dubbed Web 2.0—but most of these were really closer to media companies. The hard work was no longer technical, which had always been the Valley's forte; it was amassing large audiences and innovating new advertising models to sustain them.

Many people hoped that cleantech could be the new computer, and indeed Barack Obama talked this up in his 2008 Presidential debates as a way to fix the economy. There were plenty of opportunities to change the way we use and generate electricity, and done correctly it could be a huge market. But cleantech represented two things venture capitalists hate: investing in so-called science fair projects where hundreds of millions could be spent before you'd even know if you had a product, and having to be dependent on the government. There was inevitably going to be a few decades where the costs of remaking our electrical lives would be prohibitive for most consumers, and hence would have to be subsidized by something like tax incentives. A lot of VCs talked a good game about cleantech, but most of the investments were lower-capital plays that only nibbled at the core problems, like a software system for better routing electricity around large retail chains.

A glaring exception was Elon Musk, one of the founders of PayPal and an immigrant from South Africa. While his fellow PayPal alums plowed their money back into the Web 2.0 world—funding or starting companies like Facebook, LinkedIn, YouTube, Slide, and Yelp—Musk built a rocket company called SpaceX, a solar panel company called SolarCity, and an electric car company called Tesla. He invested more than $180 million of his own money in these ventures, and much of the world thought he was stark raving mad.

Indeed, calling Musk eccentric is an understatement. He's got a laugh like a James Bond villain and a flaring temper to match, and he's wildly unpredictable. Just after eBay bought PayPal for $1.5 billion, he reportedly wrecked a brand-new McLaren S-1 on Silicon Valley's windy highway 280. He doubled over in laughter by the side of the road. Why? He hadn't yet bought insurance on the car. He stands out all the more because this kind of entrepreneur is so unique in the Valley right now.

The Curse of Short-Term Thinking

I asked Musk once if he was crazy. How could he think that he—a computer guy—could build an electric car company when General Motors had invested $1 billion on the EV1 only to kill it off? "I didn't really approach this thinking it would be the best rank-order return on investment," he said. "If I thought that I'd be pretty crazy. I just thought it was pretty important for the future of the world." Meanwhile, in Silicon Valley, VCs hem and haw over investing in a company like Facebook at too high of a valuation, because they can't immediately determine how they'll double their money. This is the curse of short-term thinking. It's not risk-based investing if you can see an exit before you do the deal. Or as legendary venture capitalist Vinod Khosla sums up his industry's sad evolution: "There's too much capital and not enough venture."

In the early days of venture capital, VCs were nothing more than a collection of ex-entrepreneurs and frustrated bankers who made bets on intuition and relationships. They didn't have to see a market to invest; they didn't even have to see a product. "They were willing to bank on intuition and trust, combining patience with an understanding that it might take five to seven years for them to see a return," writes ex-Valley entrepreneur Judy Estrin.[1] This went hand-in-hand with government spending on long-term, high-risk research—the kind of research that helped create the Internet. The government funded the development of the Internet for a stunning 24 years. If the Advanced Research Projects Agency (ARPA) network and government research was as robust now as it was in earlier decades, the United States would be a leader in cleantech, and private and public market returns would have followed.[2]

This is a direct trickle down from Wall Street and the result of large pension funds, fund-of-funds, and endowments becoming the backers of VCs, not wealthy individuals and believers in the long-term benefits of true innovation. Wall Street lives its life quarter to quarter, and the ability to closely track stocks and funds online, on CNBC, and even on your smart phone encourages this. There are a few public-company CEOs who have the credibility and confidence to stand up to this pressure, among them Steve Jobs of Apple, Jeff Bezos of Amazon, and Larry Ellison of Oracle, but the list is short. If startups continue to act like public companies, Silicon Valley is in big trouble.

Publicly held tech companies talk a good game about their investments in R&D, or research and development, and indeed the investment in company-based R&D has soared. In the 1970s, it surpassed government-sponsored research for the first time, leading the government to think private enterprise didn't need groups like ARPA anymore. But the reality is that most of the company-led research is mostly "D" and barely any "R."[3] That may help the balance sheet and stock price in the short term, but it robs the company long term. Google gets high marks for requiring that its engineers spend 20 percent of their time on new projects. Unfortunately, many engineers at Google will tell you that math is based on them having 120 percent time.

By contrast, Estrin describes the glory days of Bell Labs, a division of AT&T that helped discover revelations in the field of chips and transistors—the Petri-dish elements that would eventually drive decades of high-tech growth in the United States. The scientists at Bell Labs worked on whatever they wanted. The incentives to invent weren't based on how commercial they could be, but rather they were based on how much scientific acclaim the scientists got from peers.[4]

Indeed, the more big, publicly traded tech companies have talked about innovation, the more they've just bought it rather than invented it. Cisco Systems, Microsoft, Google, Yahoo!, eBay, and Oracle all nailed one core product that made them tech giants and then bought their way into secondary products in order to continue to show Wall Street growth. Contrast that to Apple, which followed up its iMac success with the iPod and the iPhone, or Amazon, which leveraged its success in ecommerce to become a cloud computing vendor and consumer electronics company with the Kindle book reader.

This is the flip side of the great wave of tech initial public offerings (IPOs) in the late 1990s. Their natural growth has run its course, and a Wall Street dominated by activist hedge funds and short-term investors expects more—now! Developing products and new markets from the ground up doesn't deliver that. What does? A big acquisition that can send the stock soaring and blur year-over-year organic growth rates.

There are a lot of dangerous ripple effects from this approach for the Valley's startup ecosystem. When you have a cast of willing buyers, it incentivizes entrepreneurs and VCs to build products— not companies—that can be flipped early and often. Worse still, it rarely helps customers. While companies talk about buying innovation, they have a shoddy track record of incorporating and investing in what they buy. In some cases, the deal is less about buying a good product and more about taking a potentially disruptive competitor out at a cheap price. Either way, entrepreneurs usually wait out their vesting period, after which they are free to leave and start something new. That cycle, in turn, hurts the Valley ecosystem, because you have fewer entrepreneurs who are experienced at really building and running a business.

⚮

Too Little Reward

Some structural problems have also forced the Valley to become more mercenary and short-term focused. After the 2000 bust, the U.S. government passed something called the Sarbanes-Oxley Act, which created a host of new rules for public companies. The goal was greater transparency and accountability, and it included things like deeper audits and forcing CEOs and some board members to personally sign documents that earnings and other announcements were legitimate, to avoid their passing the buck in the case of another Enron-like situation of outright fraud.

Like most reactionary legislation, however, Sarbanes-Oxley had a host of unintended consequences. For one thing, some of the most qualified people no longer wanted to serve on public company boards because of the new personal liability involved. Even worse was the costs entailed in Sarbox compliance. Suddenly, being a public company cost millions more, which dramatically froze the ability for fast-growing but cash-strapped companies to go public. The only real beneficiaries were accountants, insurance salespeople, and lawyers.

Wall Street banks, too, developed new rules and policies that chilled small cap IPOs. Stricter lines were drawn between analyst research and banking. Again, the intentions were good: In the late 1990s, favorable analyst coverage was frequently traded for the rights to take a company public. But by untethering the two, research began to focus only on the large cap names that the greatest number of customers and traders would care about. Suddenly, smaller companies were completely uncovered, which dramatically decreased investor interest in their stocks. Without trading volume, a public company might as well still be private. Insiders and investors couldn't sell off shares without buyers, making returns just as elusive. Companies couldn't use that stock currency for acquisitions, nor could they tap the market again for more stock or bond money to grow their businesses.

Finally, there were no boutique banks left to champion these smaller deals. In the early formative decades of Silicon Valley, there were four boutique firms known for ferreting out hot companies, taking them public, and making outsized returns for their investors. They were Alex. Brown, Robertson Stephens, Montgomery Securities, and Hambrecht & Quist. During the IPO bubble of the 1990s, each of them was acquired by a bulge-bracket Wall Street firm. When the Valley crashed, Wall Street fired a lot of those local San Francisco deal makers. A few boutiques tried to start up again—some even lead by the same guys who started those four early firms—but with the new structural problems curtailing the smaller IPOs that had built their earlier empires, they didn't have the same success.

Because much of NASDAQ appreciation in past decades had come from new, disruptive companies, curtailing the ability for them to go public also hurt the overall appreciation of the market. Put another way, if everyone's retirement is locked up in the same large cap companies like Microsoft and Google, there's not a lot of room to beat the market and make money. Without public-market investing, the goings-on in Silicon Valley are just that. One could argue that these changes on Wall Street are at the root of many of the problems with risk-taking and short-term thinking in the Valley. Simply put: Taking big risks doesn't work when there's no reward. If the only reasonable exits are acquisitions, then why should investors or entrepreneurs invest the time and money to build a big business?

In 2009, Grant Thornton released a study called "A Wake-up Call for America"[5] aimed at calling attention to these structural problems with the public market. Researchers emphasized that the only way to make money today was by using sophisticated high-frequency trading. That's just what we need: a market already wrecked by a fixation with the short-term becoming even more short-term obsessed. "Our one-size-fits-all market structure has added liquidity to large cap stocks, but has created a black hole for small cap listed companies," said David Weild, former vice chairman of NASDAQ and capital markets advisor at Grant Thornton. He continued: "Wall Street's very nature has been substantially transformed."

Because those IPO returns helped create the Valley in the first place, the Valley was substantially transformed along with it. The number of U.S. listed companies has declined more than 22 percent since 1991. The study argued that the United States needs 360 new listings per year just to replace the listed companies that go away every year, whether through acquisition, going private, or bankruptcy. Wall Street hasn't seen numbers like those since 2000.

Pascal Levensohn, an investor with Levensohn Venture Partners and board member of the National Venture Capital Association, doesn't sugarcoat the implications for U.S. entrepreneurship. He said at the time of the report, "(This) inhibits job creation and hurts American entrepreneurs more than any other group. If we can't repair the bridge into public markets, the next generation of innovative private enterprises—starved for long-term risk capital in the U.S.—will continue to move to non-U.S. emerging innovation hotspots, where startups are nurtured through attractive capital incentives."

Venture capitalist Bob Ackerman puts things more bluntly, "We're dismantling the reward side of the equation. This isn't about VCs having sour grapes. We'll be just fine. I can invest in India and China. Talent and capital are the two most mobile assets in the world. They'll go to where they are welcomed and rewarded. This is about the decay of U.S. innovation."

Even President Obama broke from the traditional America-is-the-best-country-on-earth rhetoric in his January 2010 State of the Union speech to address the fact that complacency was holding the United States back. He stated, "China's not waiting to revamp its economy; Germany's not waiting; India's not waiting. These nations, they're not standing still. These nations aren't playing for second place. They're putting more emphasis on math and science. They're rebuilding their infrastructure. They're making serious investments in clean energy because they want those jobs."

Estrin echos with this statement: "Great companies often fail when they take their success for granted. And so, too, can great societies."[6]

It bears noting that this topic of entrepreneurs and investors increasingly playing it safe gets a lot of intense debate at the senior levels of power in the Valley. But the debate isn't whether or not this derisking and move to smaller, more certain outcomes is happening.

The debate is whether it's necessarily a bad thing. Many entrepreneurs see nothing wrong with aiming to build a $100 million business or designing a product that can be flipped for $20 million. Not everyone, they argue, wants to or needs to build a huge public company, especially given how unpleasant running one has become.

Being an entrepreneur is about following your dreams, and if your dream isn't to build the next Google, by all means, don't. But don't expect to raise venture capital or get on the cover of magazines either. And don't expect to change the world.

⋘∞⋙

If Silicon Valley were a stock, it would be Microsoft. Just as Microsoft is still the world's largest software company, so too is Silicon Valley still the largest hub of this breed of modern entrepreneurship and venture capital—and neither shows signs of that dominance changing overnight. Microsoft could fail in Web advertising, mobile phone operating systems, entertainment and video games, and its core businesses would still funnel some $60 billion in revenues into its coffers every year.

But if Microsoft's dominance hasn't been challenged, it is slowly but surely eroding in terms of influence. On platforms like the Web and mobile devices, the war isn't between Microsoft and anyone, it's between Google and Apple. Even with its dominant products, percentage points of market share here or there are increasingly going to competitors, be they Google, Salesforce.com, or Firefox. It's not the cash Microsoft is still raking in that matters, it's that shift in momentum. Customers don't get excited by a Microsoft launch anymore, many top employees have long since left to work for companies like Google and Facebook, and the stock is essentially where it was 10 years ago.

Like Microsoft, Silicon Valley won't lose in sheer numbers of startups or dollars spent, and it will probably still continue to give birth to most of the billion-dollar companies for the next decade. But, like with Microsoft, the momentum is shifting. No one stays on top forever in technology, especially in the Internet age. As the home to Davids continually toppling Goliaths, the Valley should know this better than anyplace. In short, the modern entrepreneur movement worked too well for Silicon Valley. Success transformed it from a place that was all about upsetting the status quo to a place that wanted the status quo—the bulk of the money, the best talent, and attention—to continue. Silicon Valley suddenly has everything to lose.

VCs are already shifting where they invest. Ten years ago, the most powerful VCs in the Valley refused to invest outside a 30-minute drive or one-hour flight radius of the Valley. The world had to come to them. Now, with nearly every firm in the Valley investing in Israel, India, or China, that's changed dramatically. Almost to a firm, the most senior and powerful partners are spending many weeks a year traveling the emerging world and looking for deals. It's the only way the Valley's Sand Hill Road will continue to stay at the epicenter of financing innovation—by going to markets that are actually growing and thriving. VCs aren't all investing geniuses, but when the so-called life blood of a region starts to leave, that says something.

Investing in emerging markets hasn't been easy for an industry that's always been about local deal making and clubby relationships. Firms can't rely on their sterling reputations or networks of contacts to get the best deals. They have to fight for them. And smart entrepreneurs like Rwanda's Jean de Dieu Kagabo have the home-field advantage. Many of them have the option of taking Western money, taking local money, or just continuing to bootstrap their companies—options that the first generation of American entrepreneurs never had. As a result, entrepreneurs like Kagabo are a mixture of this old-world entrepreneur and the modern Valley entrepreneur they read about online or hear about when VCs come courting.

Emerging market growth aside, if returns were still strong in the Valley and the United States, most VCs would stay put. But with their industry facing 10-year returns at or below the broader markets for the first time in its history, it's time for them to take the kinds of risks they used to demand of their entrepreneurs. It's time to find a new greenfield.

Israel

3

How Israel Became a Startup Powerhouse

I'm standing in a packed, poorly ventilated club located underground in Tel Aviv. No matter where I stand, I'm in the flow of traffic. As a result, more of my glass of wine is on the floor than in my stomach. I can barely hear what my companions are saying over the loud music and even louder talking. The cigarette smoke is scorching my eyes. I'm surprised no one is dancing on the bar. This is, after all, Tel Aviv.

"Our table should be ready soon," my host for the night, Ayelet Noff, screams to me, even though I'm standing only a few feet away. Ayelett runs a Web consulting practice she calls Blonde 2.0. Tall, leggy, and—not surprisingly—blonde, Noff is remarkably girly for an Israeli, especially compared to another fixture in the Tel Aviv Web scene, Orli Yakuel.

Yakuel is a noted blogger who knows more than almost any-one I've met about the latest, hot Web 2.0 app, no matter where in the world it has been created. She's blonde and pretty, but girly she isn't. She once told me she and her friends would get rewarded during their time in the army by getting to go jump out of planes with the boys. The army had an ulterior motive here: No boy would wimp out of the jump after a bunch of girls bounded out of the plane with glee. In Israel, it's not uncommon to see a gaggle of teenaged girls huddled together on a corner giggling just like they would in a mall in the United States. Only in Israel, they're dressed in fatigues and strapped with AK-47s. Israeli women are an intrigu-ing mix of girly and bad-ass.

"The smoke is horrible in here," I say, blinking hard.

"We just passed an antismoking ban," Ayelett says. She explains that her father, a member of the Israeli parliment, was instrumental in passing the ban, not because he's a health nut, but because her mom is a big smoker and he wanted to punish her during their recent divorce.

"That's crazy," I say. "So when does it go into effect?"

"Oh, it already has," she answers. I look around, confused.

"If the cops came in, everyone would put their cigarettes out," she explains matter-of-factly. Until then, no one is breaking any law. What cigarettes?

This reminds me of a joke that venture capitalists who invest in Israel love to tell about a pilot who is flying into Jerusalem on December 25. After he lands, the pilot comes on the PA and says, "We'd like to thank you for flying with us today. Please stay seated with your seatbelts fastened until we've taxied to the gate. For those of you still seated, Merry Christmas. For those of you standing, Happy Chanukah."

They love this joke because it's true: Israelis refuse to stay seated as a plane taxis to its gate no matter how many times a flight attendant tells, begs, or orders them to. I've seen people opening the bins and collecting their luggage during a descent and, on one occasion, a flight attendant march down the aisle, snatch a bag from an Israeli's arms, and throw it back into the overhead bin.

But investors also love this joke because it's exactly why Israelis make such great entrepreneurs. They follow the rules just as much as they need to and ignore the rest. There is no such thing as business—or life—as usual in a place like Israel, so quitting your job to build something new doesn't seem so crazy. What risk?

⚭

In the 1990s, when Silicon Valley was soaring, a lot of research was done on what makes a good hub for high-growth entrepreneurship. The common answer was a cocktail of elements, including top universities, proximity to venture investors, local professionals like lawyers and accountants skilled at serving high-growth companies, existing high-tech companies that could create a skilled workforce, and an environment that encourages risk taking and tolerates failure.

Here's the mystery of Israel: If you take out that last one about risk taking, Israel had none of these advantages and had the added disadvantages of a tiny domestic market surrounded by enemies and embroiled in near-constant violence. Yet in the 1990s, Israel experienced an entrepreneurial miracle. It was home to more NASDAQ traded companies than anywhere else outside of Silicon Valley. Even as recent as 2008, per capita, Israel got a staggering 30 times the venture capital investment in Europe, 80 times greater than China, and 350 times greater than India.[1] That alone makes tiny Israel required study for any country hoping for its own entrepreneurial miracle.

But here's the second mystery of Israel: Since the 1990s, Israel's unexpected and incomprehensible startup success has lead to an explosion in at least three of those elements listed previously. There are more than 100 venture capital firms operating in or investing in Israel right now. There's a strong local crop of skilled local bankers, lawyers, and accountants, who can get a startup up and running in a matter of days. And nearly every technology company—from Microsoft to Google to Cisco to Intel—has huge R&D centers in Israel. This isn't low-level R&D either: Israelis have come up with some of the more company-changing products, including Intel's Pentium chip.

But a curious thing happened on the way from being a place that had nothing to lose to a place everyone expected to win. Somehow, as Israel developed more of the ingredients that academics would consider crucial to high-growth company formation, returns from those startups have plummeted. According to Dow Jones Venture Source, from 2001 to 2008, venture capitalists invested a whopping $10 billion in Israel, but those investments returned a paltry $860 million in IPOs and acquisitions over the same period. Meanwhile, Europe—a place long considered too stodgy and risk-adverse for venture capital investing—returned $6.3 billion to venture investors over the same period. Sure, two-thirds of that was eBay's acquisition of Skype, but that's exactly the point: Israel had no big, single multibillion homerun of the last 10 years, just a bunch of singles and misses.

To be fair, the numbers probably don't count all of Israel's exits over the last decade. For one thing, many companies move their headquarters from Israel to the United States after raising money, so they may get counted as Israeli when they take funding and American by the time they get bought or go public. Still, the trendline is unmistakable. Even if Dow Jones is missing some exits, it's not enough to make the returns *good*.

Why has so much money continued to flow into Israel if the returns have been so bad for so long? Reason one is that venture capitalists expected Israel to perform better than it did in the 2000s. VC funds invest and reap returns over slow 10-year cycles. So where the money flows is a *lagging* indicator of the current health of a startup ecosystem.

Reason two goes back to Fred Giuffrida's slide (discussed in Chapter 2) that showed an elephant—or $1 trillion—trying to shove itself into a tiny box—or the universe of VC funds. In the post-2000s, there was such a surge in institutional money trying to flow into venture capital that any area—whether a firm, industry, or country—that had shown strong returns in the past was saturated with willing capital.

Israel's surge in willing investment after the 2000 meltdown wasn't a sign of a new start; it was the lingering benefits of the great run of the 1990s. That's why venture funding can be an unreliable short-term metric of an economy's entrepreneurial mojo. If there's going to be a shakeout for Israel, it'll only *start* happening now.

Behind the stats, local investors and entrepreneurs back up these concerns. Matt Hertz rebelled against his orthodox family by deviating from his preordained path of a lifetime of religious study to start a Web company. He always felt out of step with the traditions, the rigidity, the idea of a life shut in a room with only the Torah. But when he got to Tel Aviv, he felt just as out of step in the raging Web 2.0 scene. "There's a new breed of entrepreneur that only knew the good times of the 1990s," he says late at night after a day of coding. "There didn't use to be VCs; there didn't use to be 'exits.' There's a thin layer of real people, and there are a lot of entrepreneurs just playing the game."

Hertz hasn't raised venture funding for his person-search engine Pipl.com, because he doesn't want to be part of it all. In a crowded scene, he feels alone. "Comverse, AmDocs, Checkpoint," he says, rattling off some of the biggest Israeli hits of the late 1990s. "Those guys are all 40. They're not my age."

Michael Eisenberg is a partner with the Israeli office of Benchmark Capital, one of the top Silicon Valley venture firms. Eisenberg is an Orthodox Jew with eight kids. He shuttles back and forth between Jerusalem and Benchmark's Silicon Valley office several times per month advocating for Israeli entrepreneurs and justifying why Benchmark still needs an Israeli fund. But Eisenberg doesn't deny the reality that Israel's startup ecosystem is in serious danger. "What is clear is that venture returns out of Israel have not been stellar for the last decade," he says. "For that matter, venture returns in Europe and the USA have not been stellar either over the last decade. There is no way to sugarcoat that, and LPs are hurting from that."

Saul Klein, an investor from London-based Index Ventures, is another concerned believer in Israel. While Israel has declined, Index has had a hugely successful decade investing in stodgy old London, a place far less known for taking entrepreneurial risk. Among Index's hits are Skype, MySQL, and last.fm, which netted nearly $3 billion in returns between them. Klein puts it best when he says, "Israel is in serious danger of being a one-decade wonder."

⁓◈⁓

The keys to both the mystery of Israel's great run in the 1990s and the mystery of why its returns crumbled a decade later are found by looking at a few factors: the unique nothing-to-lose chutzpah of Israeli entrepreneurs, several smart policy moves by the Israeli government that played to the country's endemic strengths, and some stellar market timing.

Much of Israel's entrepreneurial spirit can be traced back to the requirement that most of its citizens spend two to three years in the Israeli army. At a young age, Israelis are thrust into a role where they have to make life-and-death decisions. A comparative lack of hierarchy means there's far more autonomy for the average soldier than in the U.S. Army. Israeli cadets are encouraged to question their superiors, a quality they take into the business world, onto planes, and into any club that tries to tell them they shouldn't smoke.

For Israelis, the competition and grooming to get into certain elite squadrons of the army is analogous to what Indian parents go through prepping their kids for the rigorous India Institute of Technology exams. A top nod from either ensures the best training, social standing, and career options for life.

The Israeli army teaches the art of working within constraints. There's a focus on creative problem solving that's given birth to many of the underlying technologies that drove the country's technology explosion, especially in fields like cryptography, fraud prevention, and security. It turns out that a life-or-death battle to thwart terrorists is pretty good training for fighting cyber criminals.

Unlike many Western countries' cadets, Israelis are all but guaranteed to see combat. That kind of experience, along with the general everyday combat that comes with life on a sandy strip of land surrounded by enemies, gives many Israelis an almost reckless lust for life that's especially pronounced in secular Tel Aviv. Israelis work hard, play hard, drink hard, eat hard, argue hard, and live like there's no tomorrow, because there may not be. What's the risk of starting a company compared to that? "We Israelis know that temporary is the most permanent thing there is," Hertz says. This is why investors like Klein and Eisenberg are not pulling out of Israel, despite a decade of lousy returns.

But entrepreneurship honed through the military experience wasn't the only factor in Israel's late 1990s surge. The country wisely structured things to make the most of this spirit at exactly the right time. Coming off what economists dubbed a "lost decade" between the mid-1970s and mid-1980s, Israel made several smart moves that laid the foundation for its insanely lucrative high-tech run that would result in countless millionaires and an economy that grew faster on average than the developed world for much of the last 15 years.[2] Even wars and terrorism couldn't slow the country down.

The country used the greenfield opportunity of being a relatively young state to tailor its ecosystem, laws, and policies on foreign investment and company formation to mirror Silicon Valley, eliminating some of the biggest barriers to direct foreign investment. In 1993, Israel created Yozma, a fund-of-funds with the goal of jumpstarting a local venture capital ecosystem. This was crucial, because most U.S. investors don't like to do foreign deals unless they have a local partner on the ground.

Yozma gave birth to an entirely new asset class with just $100 million. The fund co-invested—frequently with Valley firms—in local Israeli VC funds and directly in some startups. By 2005, Israel had more than 60 VC funds and $10 billion in available capital. Yozma was privatized after four years, quickly getting the government out of the business it so successfully seeded.[3] It was an amazing anomaly that sent countries as diverse as the United Kingdom, Japan, Germany, Korea, and Singapore to Israel to study what it did right. Most government-funded programs to spur entrepreneurship spend far more and accomplish little to nothing. It was the economic policy equivalent of lightning in a bottle.

An often-overlooked contributor is Israel's tolerance and encouragement of immigration, with the caveat that you have to be Jewish, of course. Implicit in the country's founding was that Israel would be a melting pot of Jews from around the world. As a result, the population has grown nine-fold in its short 60-year history,[4] welcoming everyone from Holocaust survivors to highly educated Soviet Jews to poor Ethiopian Jews who had never seen a television or a telephone and still observed the strictest tenants of the Torah. The country didn't just welcome erudite Jews; it welcomed all of them, and they were all made citizens on day one—no waiting periods and no tests. That put a big burden on the state, but as the Valley well knows, immigrants make some of the best entrepreneurs. It's as if the very people willing to take risk self-select themselves into the country.

There's a third rarely talked about reason why to date no other country has been able to replicate Israel's amazing startup success: The country had amazingly fortuitous market timing. With startups, market timing is as important to success as the product or the team. Some companies are just too ahead of their time, and some have a better product but are just too late. Israel, as a country, couldn't have timed its attention towards developing an ecosystem of high-growth entrepreneurship any better. Venture capital was getting large enough as an asset class that firms were just starting to think globally. But markets like China and India were largely still considered too primitive and too risky.

Israel played to its strengths, carving out a specialty in security and cryptography that largely spun out of the uber-high-tech, MacGyver-esque military. Even this specialty had the luck of timing, since corporate computing, security, and Internet banking were exploding with technical problems to be solved and billions to be made for those who could solve them. As all of these bets from the early and mid-1990s started to mature, in came the insatiable demand for tech IPOs of the late 1990s. As many impressive things as Israel did to encourage entrepreneurship and court foreign investment, without the general boom of the late 1990s and the ability for nearly any growing tech company to go public on the NASDAQ, the great Israeli success story would not have been nearly as great.

When you consider how much timing played a role in returns, it's no surprise that Israeli venture capital returns have declined right along with those of the United States over the last decade. Both were essentially designing technology products for a growing market that stopped growing and trying to build public companies for a market that no longer wanted to take them public. Closely tying its fortunes to Silicon Valley was brilliant in the 1990s. In the 2000s? Not so much.

But there are other reasons why entrepreneurship in Israel has faltered. Its over-reliance on the United States was necessary to tap into a market large enough to build a big company, but most of these U.S. investors insisted that Israeli companies move their headquarters to the United States too, just keeping R&D in Israel. This meant Israelis got better at training a technology workforce but were never pushed to develop skills like management and sales.

Israel basically turned its entrepreneur-created companies into U.S. multinationals with Israeli R&D hubs. Israel created the companies, then willingly made itself an outpost. It outsourced its own *highest-level* jobs to the United States.

Within the country, experts are divided on whether this was a mistake. Israeli companies could never have gotten so large if they'd tried to serve markets like the United States and Europe with an Israeli sales and management team, some argue. Yes, they gave up a lot, but think of the billions that flowed back to the country when those companies were able to go public or sell for high valuations. That may be true, but it means this startup nation doesn't really have an independent tech economy.

Given this pattern, the lack of a local market, and the lack of local management expertise, many Israeli entrepreneurs just aim to sell their companies from the start. In other words, in terms of risk taking, Israel—like Silicon Valley—has in part become a victim of its own success. The more people have seen how quickly and easily writing code can turn you into a millionaire, the more people who rush into that ecosystem are looking for a quick flip. Or as Shai Agassi, one of those 1990s-funded Israeli millionaires, puts it: "They've got Shai Agassi disease."

Agassi was a quintessential Israeli whiz-kid who started coding at the age of seven. He and his father started TopTier Software, which SAP—one of the largest business software companies in the world—purchased for some $400 million in 2001. Agassi is a typical Israeli—brash, arrogant, and brilliant. At SAP he rose quickly, shaking up the staid German ranks, and at 39 years old, Agassi was picked to be the company's co-CEO. That promotion would have made him one of the highest-ranking, most powerful Israelis in tech. Instead, Israeli Prime Minister Shimon Peres talked Agassi into building Better Place, Agassi's ambitious vision of a grid of swappable battery stations for affordable electric cars.

Thanks in part to Peres' support, Israel is the early test market for Better Place. It is a small enough country that the company can afford to build a comprehensive network of charging stations, but it is large enough to be a meaningful example. Because Israel is surrounded by hostile neighbors, there's a limit to the distance the owners of the new cars would be driving. Even though his early market and many of his engineers are Israeli, Agassi has headquartered the company in Silicon Valley.

The symptoms of so-called Shai Agassi disease are the opposite of that kind of near-insane risk taking. He uses the phrase to describe kids who start businesses in the hopes of getting the kind of windfall he got from TopTier Software. People who set out to build a product, not a business; people who think small. It's a serious indictment for Agassi to levy, since the main advantage Israeli entrepreneurs possessed in the 1990s glory days was a willingness to take big risks. Nowhere is it more pronounced in Israel's startup cluster than in the consumer Internet realm. Only there, it would be more apt to call it Yossi Vardi disease. And unlike Agassi, Vardi doesn't think it needs to be cured.

Vardi is the godfather of the Israeli Web scene. Back in 1996, he seeded his son and a few friends' attempt to build an open messaging platform in the very early Internet days called ICQ. It grew like wildfire, eventually getting acquired by AOL for $407 million in cash.

The biggest gripe you hear from entrepreneurs in Africa, South America, India, and even Europe is the lack of angel investors, people who take the first early-stage risk in a company and provide immeasurable benefits in terms of guidance and introductions. A healthy angel scene isn't necessarily correlated with wealth; many successful businesspeople just don't want to back unproven teams with an unproven idea.

So it's admirable how dedicated Vardi was in seeding countless Israeli Web startups, in good times and bad. He calls it "profitable patriotism" and views the investing as about far more than money. Vardi is a cheerleader of the Israeli startup, insisting at conferences that people offer only positive, nurturing feedback. He likes to say that the people doing the criticizing are frequently the least informed people in the room. "That's what separates messiahs from the rest of us," he says of haters.

Vardi is like the warm, funny Jewish grandfather you never had, and would-be entrepreneurs and the Silicon Valley elite both generally adore him. But his kid-gloves approach is curious in a place that's known for openly questioning everyone, whether in business or the military, especially since that willingness to question everything is frequently enumerated as one of the country's great entrepreneurial strengths.

There's something else curious about the way Vardi invests. He fervently believes—and has made millions off the belief—that Israelis can compete with the Valley or anyone else on products, but they won't build the next Google. He compares Israeli Web startups to tomato farmers planting seeds. Their job is to nurture and grow tomatoes that they'll then sell to stores. The stores, though, sell to the customers. In the Web world, these stores are companies like Google, Yahoo!, and Microsoft, and Vardi has sold companies to nearly all of them.

To people who say Israel benefited in the late 1990s because of its focus on being the United States's outsourcing post for R&D, Vardi's belief makes sense. But to those who believe that constraining a country to just being an R&D outpost devalues the intelligence of their workforce, Vardi could be hurting the country's potential venture returns and jobs. This is especially true, given how the consumer Internet has changed in the last 10 years. ICQ was started at a time when fewer than 20 million Americans had Web access, let alone the rest of the world. By definition, any idea that did well back then was not only innovative; it was technologically ingenious. But companies like YouTube, Facebook, Digg, and Twitter—the darlings of the so-called Web 2.0 movement—don't draw their strengths from sophisticated technology. They are really closer to media companies.

Most of these companies win by sophisticated design, rapidly iterating on features, and getting wide enough distribution that they can create lucrative advertising businesses. None of that plays to Israel's strengths. "Israelis hate A/B testing," said Gilad Japhet, of Web startup MyHeritage. A/B testing is when Web developers put out two versions of a site and measure which one is more popular with users. "It's against our nature. We want it to be perfect before we release anything." That's anathema to the trial-and-error, user-influenced Web 2.0 movement.

Israeli's troubles with the Web have a name in Tel Aviv—fairly or unfairly—and that name is MetaCafe. MetaCafe was YouTube before YouTube existed, only it didn't move fast enough, didn't spread quickly enough, and didn't have those cozy connections that helped score YouTube a $1.6 billion purchase from Google. Now based in Palo Alto, MetaCafe is still a going concern, but it would be lucky to get an exit one-tenth of the size of that YouTube deal. MetaCafe was striking evidence for Israelis that the so-called first mover advantage that was so heralded in the early land-grab days of the Web just wasn't that important anymore.

Has the MetaCafe curse discouraged Israeli entrepreneurs from trying something new? Something has. All too often the Web ideas coming out of Tel Aviv are just rip-offs of Valley companies without much localization and only incremental improvements. It's possible that many of these Israeli iterations of Facebook and Twitter may have better features and the technology behind them. But in the simple, entertainment, design, and user-generated, content-driven Web 2.0 world, users just don't care. When it comes to the consumer Internet, Israel is chasing what's become a hot market, rather than leading like it did with security software in the late 1990s.

To be fair, that sale to Google or Yahoo! can be life-changing for the entrepreneurs, not only in terms of cash but also with a job at one of these U.S. Web behemoths. And it can make an angel investor like Vardi a nice return before a venture investor could come in and dilute his stake. But at a macroeconomic level, the pattern of selling quickly lessens the jobs an idea could create and continues to constrain development of an Israeli managerial class that could make the ecosystem truly sustainable and not overly dependent on the United States. "Israel has become an angel investor's dream and a venture capital wasteland," says Klein of Index.

As one of the most respected angels and VCs in Europe, Klein knows something about the distinction. He finds it so bedeviling that he's moving to Israel for a year to watch Web companies up close and figure out exactly why there have been so few successes. He's got a good feeling about one—genealogy site MyHeritage. It could be the only large social networking company to come out of Israel for a few reasons. MyHeritage plays to Israel's unique strength as a melting pot with a huge diaspora. Gilad Japhet has aggressively acquired smaller companies that had strengths MyHeritage didn't have, and he is literally and figuratively far from the epicenter of flashy Tel Aviv life.

∽

MyHeritage is based in a rustic farmhouse that was once owned by German Templars in a town called Bnei Atarot. If you can find the town, you can find the company. There are more chickens than people there. The founder, Gilad Japhet, is an interesting mix of friendly and intense, humble and arrogant. With his chutzpah, stubborn determination, and inclination to solve a problem with technology rather than design and glitz, he's about as old-school Israeli as you can get in an entrepreneur. He couldn't be more alien to the typical hip, young Yossi Vardi followers. For one thing, he's not selling this company. These are his tomatoes. Back off, Silicon Valley.

MyHeritage may be one of the most promising social networks you've never heard of. At the time of writing of this book, it had more than 500 million profiles on its site and some 50 million registered users. Nearly 1 million photos are uploaded to the site *daily*. MyHeritage's goal is to be the third leg of the social networking stool. Facebook organizes people's school and personal life, LinkedIn organizes people's professional life, and MyHeritage— and its competitors—want to organize far-flung, sometimes undiscovered family members.

MyHeritage was started at a time when only old people and hobbyists cared about genealogy, but several different trends have changed that. Not only has the connection-based social Web exploded, but whole databases of ancestry links have come online. The amount of family media has exploded thanks to digital cameras and video cameras being embedded in nearly every device, and technology for facial recognition software and other discovery tools for mediums like photo and video have emerged as well. Smartphones, laptops, and tablets have made it so that nearly every member of the modern family is connected all the time. Suddenly, everyone could be an armchair genealogist with the aid of all this software and a little effort.

Japhet didn't see any of this coming nearly a decade ago when he started the company. Japhet wasn't even really aware he was starting a Web company back then. He was simply tired from his own corner of Israel's go-go 1990s, he took a break from work, and he decided to dust off an old hobby he'd always loved: geneaology.

Genealogy is popular in Israel, because it's a nation of immigrants, and there's a massive Jewish diaspora around the world, but it's considered a serious academic hobby. Japhet compares it to a detective story, albeit a somewhat nerdy one. You get a tiny bit of information—maybe just a last name or a first name—and you have to discover the rest by interrogating relatives, looking at graves, and digging through dusty archives.

At 33 years old, Japhet took several months off work to travel around Europe with a laptop and a scanner, hunting down relatives and scanning in their photos. As he gathered more and more data, he looked for software that could help him make sense of it and maybe even automate parts of the painstaking process, but he couldn't find any. That idea nagged at him until he decided to build it himself. He thought the project would only take a year, and once it was built he would be a one-man shop selling and updating this software, making a decent living. Then, he told his family, he'd get a real job again. He never did.

MyHeritage was released not as a Web product but as free, downloadable desktop software. Japhet spent his savings building it, even remortgaging his house. By 2005, enough people had downloaded the software that a broke Japhet tried to raise some capital, but he didn't make such a good impression on the Tel Aviv venture set. The most he could raise was $1 million from two angel investors at a terrible valuation that left him with a small stake in the company.

As the Web 2.0 movement got going, Japhet started to get well-funded, sophisticated competitors. The most formidable one launched in January 2007, started by a well-connected Valley entrepreneur named David Sacks. The site was called Geni, and it had barely been operational when it announced that it had raised money at a shockingly high $100 million valuation.

Japhet was floored. For seven years he'd been telling the world what a great opportunity genealogy was, all the while having to scrimp, save, and give up most of his equity to keep his company in business. Here came a guy who knew nothing about genealogy and had a brand-new site worth $100 million? The company was two months old! How was that possible?

It was possible, because it was Sacks, a well-connected member of the so-called PayPal mafia. The former founders and executives from PayPal had their fingerprints all over the burgeoning U.S. Web 2.0 movement. They had founded LinkedIn, Slide, Yelp, YouTube, and now Geni, and they had invested in Facebook, Digg, and others.

Sacks had two big advantages—he knew how to turn the wonky academic science of genealogy into a sexy social Web application, and he knew how to play the venture game. He told me at the time of the deal, "Charles River Ventures invested $10 million with a double liquidation preference." That meant CRV got the first $20 million out of any exit. "Do you really think we won't even be worth $20 million? Worst case they double their money." It was an argument Japhet could barely make sense of, much less *make* to potential investors.

While Geni's whopper of a deal did a lot to validate this market, Japhet and his investors could only think of one thing: the MetaCafe curse. The Israeli Web scene had seen this movie before, and this time the well-funded U.S. competitor was from the PayPal mafia again! In the Web 2.0 world, better usability beats better technology—*every time*. And it was looking like Israelis just couldn't cut it in this new design-centric world.

If MyHeritage was going to make it, Japhet was going to have to figure out how to make an attractive, intuitive Web site—and fast. He raised some $15 million more in venture capital and acquired three smaller genealogy companies steeped in the Web arts of user experience, so-called virality, and design. In the end, MyHeritage did what MetaCafe and so many other Israeli Web 2.0 companies couldn't. Within a year, it had hundreds more profiles than Geni, more languages, and far more sophisticated technology, and it has only widened its lead since. Sacks soon founded another company called Yammer, all but admitting Geni's defeat. As an added bonus, MyHeritage finally turned profitable at the end of 2009.

What had started out as a hobby had taken over Japhet's life, threatening his marriage, his finances, and at times his sanity. "I had this endless optimism. I'd get slapped in the face 20 times and keep getting back up," he says. "This was becoming my life's work. I was not going to sell." In more than a month I spent reporting in Israel, Japhet was one of the only Web entrepreneurs I met who considered his company his life's work. That attitude is one of the biggest reasons why Japhet was finally able to raise money from two of Europe's top investors: Klein's firm Index and Accel Partners, who funded Facebook and, as coincidence would have it, MetaCafe.

Beyond MyHeritage, the consumer Internet does have some other bright spots in Israel. Ironically, one of the biggest is also the quietest—online gambling and porn. This may be surprising for a country where citizenship is defined by your religion, but many Jews don't have the same puritanical hang-ups as some people in the West do, and that has given them a big opportunity to build sites that couldn't be built in Silicon Valley, at least legally.

There's a reason Israelis have succeeded at building these types of companies: they're incredibly difficult to build technically because they are magnets for fraud and hacking. This experience draws on Israel's past as an encryption and security hub with a naughty twist.

But these are the exceptions in this consumer Internet wasteland. Mostly, Israeli entrepreneurs and investors are struggling for an industry that will make them relevant again, more than a one-decade global wonder. Israel's best hope may be a foray into a whole new audacious industry—one that combines the best endemic characteristics of the nation and forces the world to pay attention to the country once again. Movies, perhaps?

∝◈∝

"Come and look out my window," Erel Margalit said coyly. We were standing in his corner office with big pane windows covering the wall behind his desk. I walked over and peered out onto a chain of low white buildings with a courtyard in the middle. He was pointing out the animation studio, the performing arts center, and a site where a new restaurant was going in. It felt a bit more like I was standing in 1950s Hollywood than a few steps from the Old City of Jerusalem.

Margalit is the founder of Jerusalem Venture Partners. In the heyday of Israeli's tech boom, JVP was known as a communications powerhouse, founding a host of now publicly traded companies, and Margalit was one of the few Israelis to make Forbes annual "Midas List," which ranks the best VCs in the world.

Back in 2008, when I came to Israel and met with Margalit, he was in different offices that looked more like a VC's offices should—all conference rooms and white boards. But these new offices—in an old building that used to house the British Mint—were much different and much grander. Margalit seemed to have changed in the year between our meetings as well. He was more laid-back, more casual, and smoother—more, well, Hollywood.

This big transformation started in the mid-2000s. Margalit saw that the enterprise and communications boom was done, and he had decided to take things in a very different direction from the just-like-Silicon-Valley-only-better! Web set. He was going to build a highly technical Jerusalem version of Hollywood. After all, he points out, Jews are so omnipresent in Hollywood that it's a well-worn cliché. "I don't think our competitive advantage is in partnering with Silicon Valley anymore. I think it's with New York and LA." He smiled slyly and added, "We've become their friends."

Margalit clearly doesn't suffer from Shai Agassi disease. This vision isn't merely to create a new company; it's about creating a whole new industry for Israel. The biggest project is called Animation Lab, and it's akin to a more technically advanced Pixar. It's a long-term bet, because the first movie will take three to five years to produce. But that's not all. The Animation Lab will also give free and cheap six-month courses to train future employees, and Margalit has also backed a virtual world infrastructure company that allows fans to interact in the world of his animated movies, extending the franchise. He's even funded the adjacent performing arts center where cutting-edge dance, music, and theatre groups that have no other venue can perform.

It's all an effort to tap into Israel's creative class or, in some cases, to manufacture one out of whole cloth. All of this is taking place miles away from hip Tel Aviv, in a place that's known for old-world religion and new-world religious strife. "People ask 'How can Israel do this?'" Margalit says. "We're part of a people who tell stories to the world. It's about reconnecting to the tribe and bringing in new technology." Indeed, the best-selling book of all time, The Bible, did largely take place outside of his window. The mission has been an inspiration to some on staff who call the project nothing less than a new form of Zionism. Adds Margalit, "Most of us would walk through walls for this project."

Not everyone is quite so effusive, however. To a lot of Israelis, Margalit is locked in a midlife crisis, destructive, or just plain nuts. Some blame him for "blowing up" what was one of the very first Israeli venture firms. But no matter what you think of him, Margalit isn't all talk. Since changing directions, he's closed on a $100 million new media fund. I ask if he thinks his colleagues consider him a bit radical. He stops eating his salmon and wild rice, smiles, and softly says, "I hope so."

Their first animated film is called "The Wild Bunch," and it's about some warring plants that have to share the same plot of land. You don't have to be a religious studies major to guess where he drew his inspiration. Just outside his office in the old city of Jerusalem, Jews, Muslims, and Christians fight over this Holiest of Holy Lands. The movie is still in production, but the footage in progress is impressive, and the all-star cast includes Abigail Breslin and Willem Dafoe. Willie Nelson provides the voice of an elderly sage plant.

Unlike other forms of movie-making, animation uniquely plays to Israeli strengths and makes up for its weaknesses. Because an animated movie can be created virtually across geographies, Margalit can tap into that connected Hollywood Jewish diaspora more easily. He can even get big-name stars to be in his films, because they can do the voices back in studios in Los Angeles. And, of course, cutting-edge animation needs cutting-edge technology. In one swoop, Margalit is trying to create a new industry and give the old one a new reason to exist. How's that for profitable patriotism?

⌒∞⌒

Other Israelis, like Agassi, are turning to cleantech as the new hope. After all, it plays to Israel's uniquely endemic strengths. The country is replete with the main ingredients for solar power—sun, sand, and a knack for solving difficult technical problems. Israel has another edge when it comes to cleantech: It's difficult to find a place much more determined to reduce its dependence on Arab oil. There's something poetic about Israel creating the next wave of innovation that could erode its enemies' revenues.

As these examples show, audacious ideas aren't dead in Israel; they're just out of fashion. One huge hit could do a lot to revive the nation's entrepreneurial focus and acumen. Benchmark Capital's Eisenberg argues that while the last decade of results for Israeli startups has been weak, past performance is not an indication of future results. The best run-up in Israeli entrepreneurship came when no one was expecting it; the worst period was when everyone was expecting even more. There's something freeing about those expectations being down again.

Eisenberg argues that it's likely the best time to be investing in Israeli startups, especially as many Israelis focus less on serving a U.S. audience and turn their attention on growing markets in Asia and Eastern Europe. If Eisenberg is wrong, this once-unstoppable startup nation risks sliding into irrelevance in an increasingly global entrepreneurship ecosystem.

Israel proved that an almost intangible spirit of risk taking could make up for limitations like market size and access to capital. So what happens when you apply a spirit of risk to a domestic market with 1.3 billion people? You get modern-day China. Unlike Israel, China doesn't have to depend on the United States or Silicon Valley's money to take off.

China

4

Deng Xiaoping, for the Win

$\mathcal{I}$t's a balmy May Saturday night on one of a dozen rooftop
bars in between the Drum and Bell Towers. New York native
Yan Zhang is in his element. Wearing a crisp white shirt neatly
tucked into his low-slung jeans, Zhang is introducing his dozen or
so friends—again. He's excited and slurring his words just enough
to show this Saturday night has been just like any other in Beijing.

This friend works for CNN, this one works for the embassy,
this one works for the government, this one is a teacher, this one is

getting his graduate degree, these three just finished running a marathon a few hours ago, this one (the loud, flirty one) is a paralegal, this one, this one, and this one are all starting or working for tech startups. Zhang himself is starting a VC-backed company called Meiloo—a Chinese healthcare portal that helps locals navigate the sometimes-shady but fast-growing world of elective surgery. In China, two of the most popular surgeries are breast implants and eye-widening. Meiloo means healthy and beautiful in Mandarin, and most of Zhang's friends are just that.

The gang has practically flash-mobbed this bar, taking over half of the couches and chairs on the roof. They are chatting, flitting between tables, laughing loudly, and, of course, drinking. The atmosphere is festive, happy, youthful, and electric. It's a group that feels they can take on the world. They have that air of people who are certain they are in exactly the right place at exactly the right time. They are invincible. And almost every single one of them is white, American, and exceedingly well-educated. More remarkable is that every single one of them speaks effortless Chinese.

I've seen this type of thing once before. It was not very long ago—the late 1990s to be precise—that these kids would have flocked to Silicon Valley. Now, when I'm introduced to one brunette, she scoffs derisively, "Oh, San Francisco, my *favorite* city," and her cronies laugh. It's bitchy, sure, but it's how people in San Francisco would have mocked the East Coast in 1999. Now, in the afterglow of the 2008 Summer Olympics, with tens of billions of dollars in venture capital flowing around the country seeking deals, it's Beijing's turn to laugh.

Insufferable? Some of them. Entitled? Most of them. Still living in a weird post-college life? A few. But give them credit for being opportunists, pioneers, and risk takers. This gang could have had their pick of jobs in the United States, but instead they've picked up and moved to Beijing. They aren't even expats, or people paid huge salaries and put up in corporate apartments to work for overseas branches of multinationals. Most of these kids have moved here without a job because, to them, China is the most exciting place in the world right now.

Here's the reality: Not only is there a reverse-brain-drain flowing back to the emerging world, where experienced entrepreneurs, executives, and financiers are returning to their home countries, not only has the number of foreign-born kids applying to U.S. grad schools started to decrease for the first time on record, but if this rooftop in Beijing and a few dozen like it are any indication, many of the United States's most opportunistic, risk-taking, privileged grads are increasingly leaving the United States for the emerging world, too, and especially for China.

To these people, Beijing isn't the capital of some censorship-heavy, moving-in-communist-lockstep, oppressive regime we should fear and loathe. It's the city of their dreams. No, really. For this generation, China doesn't conjure up images of Tiananmen Square and Chairman Mao. They may have studied *that China* in college, but they didn't live in a time when Americans were captivated by visceral reports of such Red horror. They know China is not a democracy. They know it doesn't have free speech. And they are well aware—from experience—that it's one of the most difficult places to conduct business in. But as these kids also know, modern China has come a long way, especially Beijing. In expat-filled Shanghai, many Chinese take American names to facilitate business. Here in Beijing, many Americans take Chinese names.

In most countries, the capital is the sleepy government town and not the place where the action is, but Beijing is unequivocally where every nerve in Chinese government, culture, industry, entrepreneurship, finance, and even art and fashion all lead back to. That's no small amount of activity given that many of the 21st century's biggest political wars—whether human rights, democracy, freedom of speech, capitalism—are arguably going to face the biggest battles in China. But when it comes to greed and business,

Beijing is something even greater. It's the bright homing beacon for the Western world's profit seekers looking to get their piece of the explosive 1.3 billion-person-strong Chinese dream.

Beijing has changed a lot in the last decade, and it's not just because of the 2008 Olympics. The name Beijing used to be synonymous with uncomfortable. Nicknamed "the bathtub," Beijing is surrounded by mountain ranges, with two rivers running through it, creating a hot, sweaty sauna of humidity most of the year and trapping a good bit of the smog and pollution from nearby provinces. A lot of the negative aspects about China get exaggerated in the West, but the pollution really is that bad, and Beijing has one of the largest concentrations of it. It's a rule foreigners learn in Beijing: When you blow your nose, don't look at the tissue afterward. Some days that gray-clouded mess on the horizon isn't the smog at all; it's one of the regular dust storms that plague the city in the few spring and fall months when the humidity hasn't given way to sweltering heat or bitter, snowy cold.

And yet, having first come here post-Olympics, uncomfortable is not a word I use to describe Beijing. The drive to keep the economy growing at 10 percent per year has lead to seemingly endless buildouts in hotels, apartments, public spaces, and infrastructure. The brand-new Beijing Airport is never full, but already the government is building another one. The floors in nearly every government, retail, or office building are so overcleaned you could skate across them in socks.

Beyond keeping the gross domestic product (GDP) on the rise, the Chinese are obsessed with long-term planning even as the influence of the instant-gratification West seeps into the younger generation. The Chinese excel at detail, process, and increasingly, making money. Many argue it's an economy built on a bubble of real estate, infrastructure projects that continually boost the domestic economy, and, until 2010, an artificially constrained currency to keep export dollars flowing. Maybe, but it is not uncomfortable. China doesn't feel like an emerging market. At least in the largest cities, it has *emerged*.

Near my hotel is a bar called the D Lounge. It's one of those places that could just as easily exist in Manhattan or Los Angeles. I head over there on my first night back in town on my second trip, and guess who I run into outside? Yan Zhang, the king of the U.S. Ivy kids. For a place as big as China, the American part of it sure feels cozy. Zhang makes sure I get in and does the round of introductions again. Some faces are new; some of them I remember from the Drum and Bell night. I last saw one of them in a karaoke bar with a whiskey-and-green-tea-sipping blonde straddling his lap, telling her they'd always be together. Now she's nowhere to be seen, and he's chatting up a pretty Chinese girl. In his defense, everyone warns you that things move quickly in China.

The bottle service is flowing, and the conversation is genial. Uncomfortable? Hardly. In this bar, where everyone is well-lit, well-employed, following their startup dreams, avoiding whatever they may have run away from back home, lack of comfort seems the last thing on anyone's mind.

This is China to them—the center of an economic boom so far-reaching that we've never seen anything like it before. And they are the West's new, opportunistic lost generation. An army of smart, well-educated, unafraid refugees flooding Beijing the way James Joyce, Gertrude Stein, and Picasso flooded Paris in the 1930s. They laugh, thinking of friends who stuck around for now-decimated jobs on Wall Street or in consulting firms, while they get to experience the most exciting, electric, high-growth, fast-changing country in the world today and do it in style and, well, comfort.

Of course, there's only one problem with all that. To nearly everyone outside this bar, this isn't the real China.

⌘

Richard Robinson—an American who found his way to China a decade ago—is working on his sixth startup in the country. Years ahead of the Beijing lost generation, Robinson wound up here at the end of a Trans-Siberian railroad whim, and he mostly stuck around because he fell in love and had two children "made in China." It's home now. Work-wise his latest company uses skilled Chinese video game artists to build iPhone games. Robinson is well connected in China's Web scene, but will he be the Mark Zuckerberg of China? No way, he says. None of these transplants will. Most Americans—and the United States—can all just hope to get a piece of this wild ride.

Part of that is because the ride is something no one can fully understand, least of all an American. China's growth isn't just about people and factories. This is a vast, diversified country that essentially stayed isolated and locked in time for a century and is now suddenly undergoing rapid modernization.

It's hard to fathom the scope of this modernization. We're talking about 1.3 billion people, some rich and most poor, but between these extremes hundreds of millions of them are quickly creating the largest middle class in the world. Unlike the United States, China is making more money than it is consuming. Despite massive infrastructure projects and a vast government-employed workforce, China has put trillions of dollars of its GDP into one of the safest investments—U.S. Treasury Bonds.

In terms of industry, China's economic growth is hardly just about government spending. Every industry you can imagine is developing at the same time in modern China. And it all started some 30 years ago with Deng Xiaoping. The powerful leader of China's communist party was known more for his practicality than for his communist dogma. In the 1970s, Deng almost single-handedly converted a then-closed, backwards, sleeping monolith into a surging 21st-century capitalist superpower.

To understand the unique pistons of the Chinese economy, think about the difference between an economy developing in *serial*—or one wave of modernization at a time, organically—and an economy where industries that should be at different stages develop all at once, or in *parallel*. When industries are started in serial, one format has some time to breathe before a more modern version starts to compete with it. Companies get lulled into certain assumptions.

Consider what happened with digital media in the United States. Television broadcasters would have never expected the phenomenon of cable television, especially the rise of original programming on HBO or F/X, let alone devices like TiVo that allow you to fast-forward through ads, the main source of revenue. What was even worse? YouTube. The threat of finding endless clips and shows for free online was worrying enough that the major networks developed a competitor, Hulu, but they still struggle with how much to give away for free. Movies and music have experienced similar threats with rampant piracy online, and the newspapers have been decimated by an always-on world where locals don't need a daily paper for sports scores, stock quotes, breaking news, or movie listings. Meanwhile, Craigslist and other sites have decimated newspapers' lucrative classified market.

Dinosaurs like these are faced with the same choice. They can destroy their still larger, legacy businesses in favor of the future, or they can hold on to them as long as they can, throwing as many legal and business grenades at the upstarts as they can muster, leaving the eventual reckoning for a future CEO. The result is the long, slow decline of industries like radio, television advertising, music, newspapers, and magazines.

This is just one example of the startup cannibalization of serial development. Think of bookstores, the automobile industry, travel agents—nearly any category that got complacent and didn't keep up with what its customers wanted or the technology. They have all suffered at the hands of a newer upstart.

But imagine that you could rebuild not only one industry but the West's entire network of industries knowing everything the world knows now. Imagine not fighting with labor unions and auto monoliths in Detroit over the inevitable move from gas-guzzling cars to something more sustainable. Imagine depending on dynamic fiber-optic cables rolled out to every home and office, rather than delivering Internet through slow, legacy copper wires. Imagine when Amtrak was being built if the United States had possessed the know-how to wire the country with high-speed trains. Imagine a Hollywood where they assumed there'd be widespread piracy and file sharing, so revenues couldn't just depend on the box office, or a music industry built on the foundation—not the curse—of people paying 99 cents per song.

That's the kind of modernization happening in the emerging world, and because China had been one of the most backward countries for so long and has such a large, ascendant middle class, the parallel development of industries is the most staggering in China. It's the ultimate greenfield opportunity in terms of scale and across a wide array of industries. That means some of the best entrepreneurs in China have nothing to do with tech, but they're using the same innovative thinking to remake the most seemingly inconsequential, unsexy businesses.

For instance, take driving schools. Chinese drivers are required to log some 60 hours of study and road time before getting a license from a school that is accredited by the government. Compare that to about 50 hours to become a pilot in the United States. As more than 10 million new cars come on the roads every year, thousands of Chinese drivers are likely going through this painful process as you read this book.

Back in the mid-1990s, Xu Xiong was one of them. He was shocked at how he was treated by the driving school and its instructors. The lessons were already expensive. It was a big investment, and Xu, a hotel clerk, and his family had saved for them for months. He was going to be the first in his largely uneducated family to drive a car. Except for one problem: He didn't have money to shower the instructors with gifts like the richer kids. He refused to do other favors like wash the cars, and he worried about how he would pass the written test since he didn't have any money to pay a bribe to the officials grading it.

It didn't matter that this was the way things were done in China; Xu thought it was wrong. He quit his hotel job in 1996 and applied to the government to open an official driving school.

In a fluke of lucky timing, the government was giving out a few remaining certifications, and Xu says he got one of the last ones. There were astoundingly no fixed costs for what would seem a capital-intensive business, which was good, because Xu didn't have any money. He ran the school out of his apartment, took prepayments for classes, and simply rented cars and paid instructors on the days he had students.

Whether it was the booming economy or his focus on treating students fairly, Xu soon needed a bigger place than his apartment. The city offered him a garbage dump just outside of Beijing if he'd clean it up first. He did, and his business continued to grow. Soon, he was training so many students a day that he could finally afford to build his dream facility.

The U.S. press often describes campuses of emerging market companies by saying they look just like any campus in Silicon Valley. It's like a pandering pat on the head to other countries' abilities to put a café and a gym on the same property where people work. But these reports frequently miss a big distinction: whimsy. China's modern-day moguls of obscure industries have made so much money so quickly that they build things they could only dream about in poorer times. Home air-conditioning tycoon Zhang Yue has a miniature Versailles on his corporate campus.[1]

The headquarters of Xu's Oriental Fashion Driving School is slightly more subtle. It has a distinctive black-and-red lacquer décor that looks like what someone in the 1950s thought a modern Chinese office should look like. You walk past an indoor koi pond to get to Xu's office, and on the grounds is a petting zoo. Like Zhang's Versailles, Xu says he just always wanted one. Geese and swans roam the grounds as well. In addition to the cafeteria, there's a convenience store, there are nap rooms for instructors, massage parlors, and a hair salon on site.

Such seeming frivolity aside, Xu's operation is ruthlessly efficient, with technology applied to save costs and provide better service in dozens of small ways. For instance, Chinese law dictates how much

time students must spend in a vehicle, but a lot of it is just famil-
iarizing themselves with the car. So because cars and instructors
are expensive, Xu built video-game-type simulators where students
could fulfill those early hours.

In the past, after lessons, students had to go to a government
office to actually take the road and written tests, but Xu has brought
it all on campus. He built cozy, air-conditioned rooms for the police
to monitor drivers. This has two advantages: The police officers are
so comfortable that they'd rather be there, and students perform
better being watched on camera, not in person. Also, when they're
separated, there is no opportunity for bribes or gifts to change
hands. And when it's time for the written test, students take them at
wired kiosks that send their scores to the government office directly.
Again, no chance for a bribe. Students either pass or fail on merit.

There are elaborate roads, including bridges and faked inclement
conditions, for students to practice on, and more wealthy students
have the option of practicing in a nicer car. Xu even has his own
bus system to pick up students. The school trains 60,000 students
per year, and with all the fees paid upfront, working capital is never
an issue. As impressive as Xu's execution has been, companies like
these—the ones you never hear about in the West—exist because of
the unique ride China is undergoing at this moment in time, taking 1.3 billion people to modernity at warp speed with all the government backing they can ask for, as long as they follow the rules.

⌒∞⌒

"Stick close to me and watch your pockets," Liam Casey mutters
to me in an Irish accent so thick he might as well be telling me to
watch my Lucky Charms. Casey—called "Mr. China" by *The
Atlantic Monthly*—has been doing business in Shenzhen for 15
years. He has some of the best business stories I've ever heard, and
I can't repeat a word of them. That's because he's a manufacturer of
accessories for some of the West's biggest brands. U.S. brands strictly
swear every Chinese company to secrecy, and Casey's company

PCH International is no different. Casey is also a fixer. He could bill thousands of dollars per hour just for his China advice if he wanted to. Instead, he gives it to potential customers for free, building his profile as "Mr. China" even more. He smiles and laughs almost constantly, but don't be fooled. Anyone who has climbed his way to the top of the Shenzhen manufacturing heap in the last 15 years has sharp elbows. As such, he's the perfect guide in this city.

Casey and I are entering the SEG electronics building—an eight-story building that would reduce the most sarcastic, too-cool-for-school Silicon Valley engineer to a pile of tears. On the ground floor, hundreds of booths display every circuit, chip, or piece of wiring you could want. On the next floor up are screens, motherboards, and connectors. Next up are crudely assembled devices, and up and up until you get to the top floor, which looks like an overcrowded Best Buy with way too many gadgets and products to chose from. You can wander through hundreds of mom-and-pop retailers, and by the time you get to the top floor have everything you need to assemble your own knock-off iPhone.

The booths are staffed by young Chinese kids with calculators tapping out what this many of this widget can fetch you. Some slump over asleep between customers. It's a familiar site. Everywhere you go in Shenzhen, you see teens slumped over asleep. But when you walk up, they spring to life. They flirt, they haggle, they cajole. There are desks of traders—à la Wall Street trading pits—who move high volumes of tech's modern primordial elements. Even in the middle of a weekday the whole place is packed. Value is literally being created on each floor as crude elements become reasonably well-built knockoffs of MP3 players, touch-screen movie players, and laptops.

It reminds me of the old diamond district in Los Angeles, where you wander from booth to booth getting barked at, haggling, and hoping to get a deal. When my husband bought my engagement ring there six years ago, an Iranian immigrant escorted him up several floors to an office with bars covering the windows. On the desk were a gun and wads of cash, and safes full of diamonds flanked the office. In Southern China, the diamonds are these high-tech building blocks, and it doesn't take long to look around Shenzhen to see there are plenty of wads of cash changing hands.

This is the geek wonderland of Shenzhen, one of the first and perhaps the most capitalist cities in all of China, thanks, again, to Deng. Shenzhen is a city of mercenaries, hustlers, and transplants looking to make their fortunes. It's as known for smokestacks and smugglers as it is for chips and motherboards. The day before I arrived, a friend in Beijing warned me that gangsters in Shenzhen ride mopeds up on the sidewalk, break your legs so you can't run, and then rob you. Generally, this is a city where you should, as Casey says, stick close and watch your pockets. "This is the only corner in the world where you've got a Dolce & Gabbana store across the street from a hot pot restaurant serving dog," Casey says just outside of his company's headquarters. "Guaranteed."

Outside SEG, there are hundreds more kiosks where you can get knockoff Nokias and iPhones. There are neon signs everywhere, only it's not really neon. Shenzhen is the home of LED production, so these signs are crisper, brighter, and more fluid than any in Vegas or Times Square. It's bright even in the daytime. As you walk from the metro to SEG, you get the regular urban series of street vendors and promoters. First they're hawking taxis, then massages, then the closer you get, it's illicit copies of Windows 7. This is the China that keeps Silicon Valley awake at night. It's also the China that makes its modern gadget boom possible.

Not far from here are all those factories that make the products we consider emblematic of modern American life—from iPods and Nikes to nearly anything sold in Wal-Mart. The armies of thousands of young women all wearing jeans and a certain color shirt streaming from dormitories to start their days making things we'll all later consume in giant cavernous factories where the conditions may not be what we'd like, but compared to life back on a Chinese farm are mostly welcome and definitely higher paying.

China is three decades into the largest migration in human history—from the farmlands to the cities, mostly seeking factory jobs. It began with Deng's agricultural reforms, which allowed farmers to sell some crops on the open markets and were meant to restore some of the productivity killed during Mao Zedong's Great Leap Forward, when farmers were forced to pool their land and crops. By the mid-1980s, farmers were allowed to legally relocate. By the 1990s, some 60 million migrants teemed through the growing cities of China.[2] China has hundreds of millions of migrant workers today, mostly in factories and coastal cities. That's three times the amount of people who flowed from Europe to the United States over a century—all in less than 30 years.[3]

Reform has changed China's rural landscape: There are few young people left, replaced instead by a flood of remittances coming home. But it is changing the makeup of the cities as well. As Leslie Chang details in her book *Factory Girls: From Village to City in a Changing China*, the motivation behind this migration has evolved. It's no longer purely about economic need or desperation. It's increasingly because these girls are bored, want to see the world, want to make something of themselves, and learn new things.[4] These girls—typically under the age of 18—are an entrepreneurial force that may not be building billion-dollar companies, but they are building their own careers, meticulously, brick by brick. They study new skills like English, explore the first tastes of independence, and climb the modern urban Chinese employment food chain by making connections, obsessing over self-improvement, and taking risks. It's a new surging economic class, never content with the latest cell phone, boyfriend, or job, always pushing for more. If these factory girls haven't hit their goals by their mid-20s, they consider themselves washed up.

It's a multibillion-dollar economy that's been almost entirely fueled by the nothing-to-lose concept. Still, this is where Chinese get the rap of being little more than assemblers and knockoff artists. And a lot of people in Southern China are happy to have the

West suffer under that illusion. Chaos is a competitive edge here. Those who embrace it and know how to navigate it can make it in Shenzhen, but even fixers like Casey never claim to understand China. The chaos can sometimes be navigated with stunning results though. Look at Barnes & Noble: The company had never produced a tech product in its life. When it decided to make an eBook reader, it came to Shenzhen, found a fixer and a factory, and within nine months they had something very close to what it took Sony years to develop.

In Silicon Valley, the network is what makes the ecosystem so powerful, especially as the region grew to rely on companies with intangible assets like software and the Web. There's a misconception in much of the emerging world that it's easy to start a company in Silicon Valley, that venture capital seems to fall from the sky. But—for all the talk of the Valley being a meritocracy—if you don't know anyone, raising money can take as long and be as frustrating as it is anywhere. VCs insist that you be introduced to them by someone they know for one simple reason: they know a lot of people, and if you can't find a single one of them to vouch for you, you're not going to be a very aggressive CEO.

Put another way, it's not your geographic location in the Valley, it's your location in the *Valley's network*. In early 2010, I was at a clubby conference in Jackson Hole, Wyoming, with 50 or so Valley elites. Between dinner and a night of drinking in the lobby, I watched a company get formed. And I don't mean an idea was sketched out on a napkin. A recently angel-funded idea raised venture capital in a matter of hours, and a lawyer on site drafted the term sheet sitting in the Four Seasons lobby. That can only happen in the Silicon Valley scene, and the Barnes & Noble example can only happen in Shenzhen.

The SEG electronics market is a physical metaphor for this kind of people-coded infrastructure: You can go to each floor buying components, and by the time you reach the top, you have enough for a prototype. This is what Shenzhen—and by extension all of

China's manufacturing segment—can do that is special. It may have started out as a cheap way to make things, but now it's a way of making things that, like company formation in Silicon Valley, simply doesn't exist anywhere else.

Like Silicon Valley, no one seems to be from Shenzhen. Deng created it out of a fishing village to be one of China's first free-trade zones, and since then it has been a Mecca for outcasts and entrepreneurs looking to create a better life—the kind of life they weren't lucky enough to be born into. That city pays Deng homage with an elevated concrete statue on a hill of him sitting lotus-style in a feng shui path that traces a line between Deng, the Shenzhen city hall—which is shaped like a giant blue stingray on stilts—and the stunningly modern library and performing arts center.

The architecture of Shanghai could be New York. The architecture of Beijing is a controlled, artsy, cutting-edge look. But the architecture of Shenzhen takes the oversized fantasy of Vegas to a new level. The Intercontinental Hotel chain is normally conservatively grand, but the bar of the Shenzhen Intercontinental is a three-story pirate ship on land. That whole feng shui line from Deng's statue, to the city hall, to the library and performing arts center and through the city is like a giant middle finger to Mao Zedong—to whom Deng owed his career but with whom he frequently disagreed. Mao hated intellectuals, creativity, individualism, conspicuous consumption, and Western-style capitalism. Shenzhen—for all its rap of being filled with assembly lines where everyone dresses alike and moves in lockstep—is everything Mao never wanted China to be, and it is especially filled with democracy-loving Americans who are here to do business.

The newest iteration of Deng's posthumous vision is a stock exchange called Growth Enterprise Board, (referred to casually in China as The Startup Board), where rapidly growing companies can go public by meeting lower revenue standards. These companies are supposed to be younger, with bigger growth potential than companies listing in exchanges in Shanghai or Hong Kong, but they are also higher risk. It took nearly a decade, but the exchange finally opened in Shenzhen in October 2009, and the country immediately saw RMB signs in its eyes.

Everything from small tech companies to paint manufacturers to burgeoning movie studios were filing to go public as soon as the Board opened, and the price-to-earnings ratios were soaring. A small panel of high-level lawyers and industry experts share the responsibility of green-lighting the companies' applications. In the early days, some 80 percent of applications were getting through. I asked one of them what a "yes" vote meant. Did it mean this company had no red flags? Or did it imply to the public that the company was a safe investment? He couldn't really answer and said wearily, "It's a lot of responsibility. We are creating new billionaires every week."

While many in Silicon Valley have begged for the creation of just such an exchange, the government and the Securities and Exchange Commission (SEC) is concerned about everyday people investing in stocks that are normally only the purview of wealthy professional VCs. They are not so squeamish in China. Communism has not only embraced capitalism, but in Shenzhen it is on global capitalism's cutting edge.

❦

"I'll have a Johnnie Walker Black on the rocks," I said, dumping a heavy purse with a camera, laptop, notebook, and history book about China onto the bar of the Sheraton Four Points, a comfortably modest hotel situated in the middle of Shenzhen's Futian free-trade zone. I'd been on the road for five weeks, visiting two continents, three countries, and nine cities, and talking to more than 100 entrepreneurs, and it had been a long day in the People's Republic.

"That's crazy. I was just about to say the same thing," said a central-casting American businessman who was walking up to the bar at the same time. Not that crazy, I thought. This was at least my 10th road trip in the last year or so, and I'd learned that "Johnny Walker Black on the rocks" was the true international language—not love or Esperanto. Sometimes it was the only bottle behind a bar, but kudos to whoever distributes Johnnie Walker Black in Asia, Africa, and South America, because they always had it, and everyone always understood that bit of English.

As the bartender poured two drinks at once, the silver-haired, blue-shirt-and-khaki-wearing man next to me said he was here representing a U.S. company that was doing a big manufacturing deal in China. I looked around at the dimly lit, faux-cherry-wood bar with faux-leather smokey-gray chairs and faux-marble-and-glass tables. It was full of men like him, huddled in conversation with their Chinese counterparts. Breakfast here is the same thing, with a different floor, brighter lights, and everyone's ordering eggs instead of Johnnie Walker Black.

"Yeah," I said. "Who isn't?"

To understand why there is not a new Cold War with China, as some U.S. politicos have alleged, look at this room. Some 20 years after Deng Xiaoping opened up the Chinese economy, the United States and China are hopelessly intertwined. Welcome to hell, Chairman Mao.

Not surprisingly, it was in Shenzhen—Deng's manufactured juggernaut of high-tech manufacturing—that I found Roy Ho. Ho's business will top $1 billion in revenues in 2011, selling mobile phones primarily to emerging markets outside of China, like India and Southeast Asia. At the time of our meeting, Ho owned 100 percent of the company, employed 10,000 people, and no one in the media had ever heard of him. Only in Shenzhen could Ho still be considered a small fish.

In a land where millions of jobs were created out of the West outsourcing its manufacturing, Ho's company, CK Telecom, is almost completely vertically integrated. That means he makes everything himself and does all of his own product design and a good deal of the product innovation, too.

Ho isn't completely alone here. Another surging company on the Shenzhen manufacturing scene is BYD, a company that started like

Ho in phones and batteries and has turned its battery technology onto solving bigger problems like electric cars and solar/wind-powered houses for China's midmarket. BYD was similarly unknown until Warren Buffett made one of his only China investments in 2008, spending $238 million to buy up as much of BYD as its CEO would let him, and suddenly catapulting the company to business-press superstardom in the United States. BYD is less focused than CK Telecom, but it has the same vertically integrated strategy.

When dogs at the dog food factory aren't eating the dog food, what should that tell other dog owners? The answer is outsourcing doesn't *always* make sense. A company in the United States can't compete with the efficiencies and cost of manufacturing in China. But if you're in China, all that low cost and efficiency is at your fingertips, so why give the control to a Taiwanese manufacturing giant like Foxconn? Instead of saving money, Ho explains that outsourcing in China would actually *cost* him margin points. Say a certain widget costs $1 on the Chinese market. That may represent 50 cents in labor and material costs and 50 cents in profits. If Ho effectively buys it from his own factory, he gets the widget and the profits. That means he can still make money in a brutal market like hardware.

BYD and CK Telecom also want to climb the pyramid—and that's what gives some Western businesspeople doing deals in the Sheraton Four Points a reason to drink. Think of the life cycle of a product like a pyramid. The top is brand: the worst Apple product still enters the world blessed. Underneath that is design: users are picky in a maturing market, and they want a device to look cool from the hardware to the user experience to even what those in device circles call the OBE or out-of-box experience. Apple excels at all three, which is a big reason no other gadget companies are mentioned in the same breath in the modern Steve Jobs era. Go down the pyramid another notch, and it gets considerably less sexy—engineering. This is the underlying technology that drives better, faster, smaller, cheaper gadgets. This is what Silicon Valley excelled at for decades, driven by the cruel master of Moore's Law, which said that the number of transistors that can fit on a chip doubles roughly every two years. Finally, underneath that is the least sexy part of the pyramid: assembly or basic manufacturing.

Assembly creates little of a product's value and is the bulk of its labor, so it was willingly given to places like China over the last few decades. And China did more than add a torrent of low-paying jobs to the problem, because many manufacturing firms innovated on the supply chain. In many cases, an order comes in from a Web site, and it goes straight to China, where a series of sophisticated lights and levers route just the right components to the right boxes, where they are shipped directly to the store or even end customer.

Right now, places like Shenzhen and Silicon Valley have a mutually assured relationship. A device company in the United States could make its own products again, if it absolutely had to, but there would be far fewer new product launches and far less innovation and capacity to fill orders rapidly. It would be expensive and painful. Likewise, China can produce products—just walk around the SEG electronics market to see evidence of that. But without superior engineering, design, and brand, they're not products the West would buy.

The problem is this may be an equal relationship in terms of *power* but not in terms of *money*. A factory in Shenzhen may keep a few dollars of a $300 product. That is why a new generation of companies like BYD and CK Telecom are climbing the pyramid. Ho's company does a lot of its own engineering now, driving innovation in areas that matter even in the mature handset business like a better camera and longer battery life. He's not quite to the design layer, but he says he will get there. Brand? "Maybe China never gets there," he says. But he adds that other than Apple, who else in today's gadget landscape consistently does?

Look at the post-iPhone world: Sure, CK Telecom sells some touchscreen copycat products, but so does Dell, BlackBerry maker Research in Motion, and Hewlett-Packard. "We're all chasing the one who has the new idea first," Ho says. "You grow in a mature market by being the one who can run faster. That's what we can do in China." He continues, standing up and doing squats, jogging in place, and doing runner's stretches in the middle of the conference room to make his point. "We have to watch and stay in the best shape so we can run the fastest."

The Chinese Communist party may have outlasted the Soviet Union, but it was only because the party—under Deng's leadership— largely eliminated anything communist from the ideology.

Deng Xiaoping, for the win.

5

Revenge of the Copycats

I am sitting in a lime green room in Xi'an with several dozen Chinese college kids. I'm wearing a metal bikini and killing bunnies with a long, Chinese martial arts–style knife. Well, the virtual me is anyway. The real me is getting stranger looks than if I were actually wearing a metal bikini and killing bunnies. Clearly, few non-Chinese-speaking Americans come in here to play games.

I'm not very good at the bunny killing. Other bikini-clad warriors keep stabbing away before I can get to them, and I don't have enough powers to go after the wolves or alligators; instead I just battle-trot through them like a ghost, looking for more unkilled bunnies. But cut virtual me some slack—she's trying to navigate an uncertain, crowded world where she is the only one who can't read a word of Chinese. The nonvirtual me is having a similar time with the nonvirtual Xi'an, a city deep in China with a "mere" 9 million people.

This room tells you everything you need to know about China's Internet revolution. It's on the top floor of a no-frills downtown office complex, and the mildewed stairwell is bedecked with game ads. The wood on each step alternates between an Intel ad and the words "GAME ON!" At the top floor is a room utterly unlike Internet cafés in Africa, India, or South America. Most of those are like simulated offices crammed together—ho-hum PCs, desk chairs, and tables. This one is more like simulated living rooms crammed together. The chairs are cozy, orange, upholstered arm-chairs, the monitors are huge, with a Webcam affixed to the top of each, and the PCs all contain state-of-the-art graphics chips.

I log onto the machine, and a flash-ad for a game splashes across the screen. The Chinese Web isn't known for its subtlety. I click past that to the desktop and see links for hundreds of games—everything from immersive, multiplayer blood-fests to the kinds of casual games you'd find on Yahoo! or AOL. People do not come here to check e-mail or apply for a job online. They are here to be entertained. They are watching pirated Hollywood movies, they are playing the bunny-killing game or a host of others, or they are absorbed in QQ—the Chinese social messaging sensation.

I sat in the VIP section, where each person gets an individual desk instead of a seat at a long table. The local Chinese businessperson never misses an opportunity to offer a VIP version of a service, which usually translates to paying more to be less crowded—a rare and valuable commodity in Chinese cities. The guy next to me was dispassionately scrolling through porn the entire time I was there. He didn't seem too moved or titillated—almost as if he was just passing the time, desensitized to a world of naked women and sex acts displayed on screen whenever he wanted them.

I tried to ask my guide diplomatically if this happened all the time in China's Internet cafés, phrasing it, "Is that a big problem here?" I meant "problem" in the sense of "epidemic." He answered, "No, it's not a problem at all. The government doesn't care about *that*." The Chinese Internet, ladies and gentlemen. And it's an Internet audience that the West needs to understand, because it is already the largest in the world, and only about 20 percent of China is online.

In the United States, the Internet started in research labs and spread through schools and offices. The Internet was a research and productivity tool first. It wasn't until the illegal music downloading free-for-all of the early Napster days that the Internet—and even computers—suddenly became cool, and it took even longer still for the Internet to emerge as a mainstream hub of Western entertainment. Silicon Valley entrepreneurs are still trying to figure out how to make money off of online entertainment. Charging for content isn't easy in a country that produces hundreds of movies, TV shows, sporting events, video games, and a million other things to occupy a bored teen's downtime. Most online media companies are just fighting for a slice of users' time and hoping more advertising dollars will migrate over from old media.

But because media development was so constrained during China's communist years, there's not a lot else for these kids in Xi'an to do. That's led to a Chinese Web that is a young, fun conduit for millions of tiny microtransactions every day. The West fixates on dramas like whether the Chinese government is censoring data on search engines, but most of these kids in Xi'an don't care. They don't go to the Web for information; they go to the Web to have fun, be entertained, show off, sound off on message boards, and connect with friends.

In the United States, the majority of people online are over the age of 30, and the largest Internet companies are Amazon, eBay,

Google, and Yahoo!—companies that facilitate transactions and provide information. In China, the majority of people online are under the age of 30, and the largest companies serve up online games.

Witness how differently something as universal as online video developed in the United States and in China. In the United States, YouTube exploded for three reasons: it was easy and browser-based, no download required; it was on the forefront of the user-generated content revolution, which piggybacked off the reality TV revolution, making instant micro-fame and attention even easier, especially since most laptops and phones came with embedded Webcams; and it gave people any copyrighted content they wanted on demand, trumping TV when it came to convenience and instant gratification.

That last one caused huge legal ramifications, which motivated the company to accept a whopping $1.65 billion acquisition offer from Google. YouTube has grown since, but product and business-model-wise, YouTube hasn't evolved much. The world never really got to see what YouTube could have become as an independent media force, and truth be told, the powerful entertainment incumbents in the United States probably would have kept that from happening even if YouTube hadn't been sold. After scores of attempts, online radio station Pandora is one of the only online music startups to escape the Recording Industry Association of America's political influence and wrath while remaining independent.

In China, dozens of online video startups sought to mimic YouTube's success, but the challenges and appeal of the sites were totally different. The two largest are: Beijing-based YouKu and it's hipper rival Shanghai-based Tudou. Most of the others died—not because of old-media incumbents or lawsuits but because they were crushed by one of the three C's of the Chinese Web: Cost, Censorship, and Competition.

The broadband costs of serving video to a nation with hundreds of millions of people online are brutal. YouKu and Tudou raised more than $100 million each in venture capital and may still need to raise more. Then there's censorship: All of the video companies except YouKu were shut down by the government at various points. Some promising ones like Disney and Sequoia Capital–backed 56.com never recovered. As for competition, even China isn't big enough for dozens of players, and increasingly the Chinese portal giants and government-controlled China Central Television have been launching their own online video sites.

Tudou and YouKu are two of the only companies I've ever interviewed that actually went through periods of trying to *decrease* their growth, because the torrent of Chinese kids coming to their sites was so crushing and expensive. It's certainly not a problem in other large emerging markets; despite the comparable population, India has about 40 million people online, and most of them access computers through work.

The numbers are hard to fathom: Every month, both YouKu and Tudou each get some 250 million unique users. That's about half what the front page of Yahoo!—the largest online property in the world—gets globally, and both could have more if they upped their broadband spending. In the summer of 2009, Tudou doubled the size of its broadband pipe, and the extra capacity was gone in a matter of weeks, says CEO and founder Gary Wang.

Tudou and YouKu have emerged to be very different things than YouTube. There aren't really dominant TV networks in China's fragmented, young Chinese media space, so Tudou and YouKu are trying to fill that void online. They ink licensing deals for TV shows and movies and increasingly are developing original scripted, reality, and talk show content for their audiences. YouKu has never been much into the user-generated content game, instead recruiting stars with the potential to produce a viral hit like a talent scout. "The Chinese people aren't really into turning a camera on themselves," says Victor Ku, the founder of YouKu. Even Tudou focuses more on would-be guerrilla filmmakers more than sheer Webcam exhibitionists.

But it's not all about virality. This throng of users flocking to these sites are largely coming from Internet cafés like the one in Xi'an, and because they are all sitting in the same room, memes, games, and videos also spread the way a fad would in the physical world. These cafés have given Chinese Web companies opportunities to market sites and games beyond buying search engine keywords, which are escalating in price in China. And one man has done a better job than anyone of tapping into this on-the-ground, almost nonviral aspect of Web marketing: Shi Yuzhu of gaming company Giant Interactive.

There are only two things I know for certain about Shi: He is very rich, and he does not, under any circumstances—no matter how many times I or mutual friends ask—want to be interviewed by a U.S. reporter. I tried for 18 months, finally scoring a meeting with Giant Interactive's CFO, Eric He, instead. Over several hours, He told me the story of Shi's life. As the only English-speaking member of the senior management team, He plays this surrogate role to Wall Street and the press a lot. Lucky for He it's a juicy story.

Shi grew up in a small town in a family with modest means in real communist China, not today's communist-in-name-only China. After working at a boring government job, Shi moved to Shenzhen, which even then was the place you could go to with nothing to make a fortune and a name for yourself. Shi wanted to start a company, and he was good at math and liked software. So he wrote a program that would translate the then mostly English-language Web into Chinese, but he had no idea how to get anyone to buy it.

A half-page ad in the *Shenzhen Daily* was 8,000 RMB—double the money Shi had managed to scrape up from friends and family. He put 4,000 RMB down and placed an ad, hoping he'd find a way to pay the rest when it ran. For two days nothing happened, and Shi was panicked. Then suddenly, he started getting orders. Shi figured if he could keep getting press, his business would grow more, and the best way to get press back in those days was to court

Communist party officials, because China Central Television cameras followed them everywhere.

Shi focused on getting them to visit his then humble one-man software shop, and as he grew his business, more of them came. In the glow of success, Shi made what he considers one of his biggest mistakes, expanding broadly into other industries like healthcare remedies and real estate. He was stretched thin financially, but his business was still growing and the press kept building.

His crowning moment of fame—and hubris—was when then Chinese premier Li Peng came to visit him. Shi had been planning to construct a new headquarters for his various businesses, first planning on a 14-floor building. Every Chinese official to visit Shi insisted he go bigger, until Li declared he should build it 72 floors, have it be the tallest building in China, and he should call it The Giant Tower. Li Peng wrote it in calligraphy on a sheet of paper, sliding it to Shi with all the gravitas of a Chinese Premier. Who was Shi to say no? Like China back in the mid-1990s, he had ambitions of grandeur that weren't quite backed up yet.

Just as Shi's business was at its broadest and most overleveraged, the late-1990s Asian financial crisis hit. Goodbye, 72-floor Giant Tower. Goodbye Giant, in fact. Shi liquidated everything he owned and drove his Mercedes—his last asset—from Shenzhen to Shanghai, selling it for as much cash as he could get when he arrived. It was just as well, because he was out of gas anyway and couldn't afford more. Shi owed 250 million RMB and refused to default on the debt as a matter of pride. The company was gone, but he vowed to personally repay every penny. It took him five years to do so, and he didn't do it with software. He did it with rebranded melatonin marketed to little old ladies in second- and third-tier cities. He called it Brain Platinum.

Shi found himself with the second daunting marketing challenge of his career. He couldn't afford to build the business in a big city like Shanghai. The several-million-person human migration was already underway, driving costs in the city as high as its skyscrapers. So he decided to market Brain Platinum to the places where that big-city money would filter back to—parents in small towns and villages. Shi traveled to 5,000 small pharmacy counters around the country, like some sort of miracle tonic slickster from an old Hollywood movie, marketing the product and building a distribution network visit by visit. By 2003, Brain Platinum repaid his debt, and Shi was back on top.

No longer fighting to rebuild his fortune, Shi became obsessed with playing Western online games marketed in China by Shanda Interactive. His favorite was Age of Hero. These games charged everyone a monthly subscription fee to play, but seniority in the game was based on how many hours users logged. Shi hated losing, but he was running a business and didn't have the time to play as much as the Internet café kids did. So he hired someone to play for him, who he paid more than Shanda's monthly subscription fee.

It struck him how much money Shanda was leaving on the table. If people like him were willing to pay to get skills and advancement faster, this could be a much bigger, more profitable business than gaming companies in China realized. He went to meet with Shanda's CEO Chen Tianqiao and told him he should offer a game free to play and then charge for power and skill upgrades. Chen was polite to Shi but mostly blew him off, so Shi hired several of Shanda's disgruntled game coders and built it himself. (Before he could launch, Shanda did launch its own free-to-play games, and much of the industry did so as well later.)

Shi shifted his attention from the Brain Platinum business to Giant Interactive, his new gaming property. He was reinvigorated, investing all of his own money in the project and obsessing over what this new game would be. Most Chinese gaming executives were more like businesspeople than gamers back then. Think of them like Hollywood studio moguls buying scripts and inking deals but not creating anything. Shi, on the other hand, was a hardcore gamer, chain-smoking and talking smack on chat boards while he played for hours at a time. Around this time, he adopted a strange fondness for track suits. "I don't really know what the deal is with the track suits, to be honest," the CFO, He says. Shi is after all pushing 50, and in his younger days he wore only suits and ties. Shi said in an interview with *China Daily*: "They just help me relax." Years later, when Giant went public on the New York Stock Exchange, Shi got special permission to wear a track suit when he rang the opening bell.

Giant's first game, ZT Online, was a massive success. There are two big reasons why. First, Shi decided that while graphics were nice, the narrative of a game was more important than mega-pixeled glitz. When a lot of analysts and competitors first viewed ZT Online, they were underwhelmed at its looks, but the narrative kept users hooked.

The second reason was Shi's innate knack for creative marketing. He used the same Brain Platinum strategy, just swapping pharmacies in overlooked second- and third-tier cities for Internet cafés. Thousands of hip gamer employees would scour thousands of cafés like the one in Xi'an every day, making sure the game was loaded on every computer, and the café staff would push ZT Online upgrades. They offer specials, training classes, and occasionally just sidle up to someone and tell them about the game. You start playing, and then you pay. Essentially, Shi built the same business twice, just swapping products and vendors. Giant went public on the New York Stock Exchange a little more than a year after ZT Online's launch.

Shi obsessively tries to learn from his personal history—whether good or bad. He's honed a marketing and distribution strategy that could only work in China's unique Internet culture. And, still bruised from his late 1990s bust, he fights the Chinese entrepreneurial temptation to go broad. That's led to one of Giant's biggest criticisms as a public company—that its revenues are too reliant on ZT Online.

Shi clearly isn't a one-hit wonder, but that doesn't mean Giant isn't one. It's been a huge compromise to convince Shi—for the

sake of investors—to release some smaller interim games, He says.
But Shi bats aside such worries, laser focused on the next (he hopes)
big hit. It should be out at the end of 2011 at the earliest, and it
will make or break Giant as a public company. It's a lot of pressure,
but then Shi has been broken before. And in modern China, there's
always a new market if this one fails.

∞

By the end of 2010, all of those gambles on the Chinese Internet
were paying off. One-quarter of all IPOs in the United States were
for Chinese companies, including Tudou and YouKu, and investors seemed to have an insatiable demand for more. Suddenly some
Silicon Valley venture funds were doing better in China than they
were in the United States, at least in the short-term.

But impressive as the numbers behind YouKu, Tudou, Giant, and
even larger Chinese Web companies like Baidu and Alibaba Group
have been, none of them are the largest Web hit in China. They are
all dwarfed by a company called Tencent. A company that makes
its revenues—as the name implies—about 10 cents at a time.

Those pennies add up: Tencent—the maker of the popular
QQ messaging platform—has annual revenues in excess of $1 bil-
lion, making it the largest Chinese Internet company in revenue
and profits. In market capitalization, it is one of the three largest
Internet companies in the world, as of the writing of this book,
after only Google and Amazon. With just under 400 million active
users—100 million more people than live in the United States—
and a $40 billion market capitalization, Tencent may be the most
important Internet company you've never heard of.

Over the next decade, that will change. Online gaming as a
whole is growing 20 percent to 40 percent per year, and Tencent
has a staggering 70 percent market share according to Carret &
Co. Equity Research. Its cuddly little penguin mascot is on nearly
every phone and PC in China and all over the company's headquarters, on lunch trays, on name badges, on cups of coffee, on

elevators. Sometimes the penguin is doing martial arts, sometimes it's fencing, sometimes it's just hanging out, but he's almost always winking as if to say, *"Don't hate me because I won."*

When I asked Tencent's chief technology officer Jeff Xiong whether the company could see itself buying a major Valley company in the future, he unblinkingly said yes. The startup negotiated with Google and Facebook on joint ventures, even though talks ultimately broke down. Tencent owns 10 percent of Mail .ru Group, the Russian investor that owns massive stakes in hot U.S. companies like Facebook, social gaming site Zynga and ecommerce deal site Groupon. Tencent even looked at buying YouTube once upon a time. So far there's little to show for a lot of negotiating. Part of that is the company's concern over diluting its culture with too big of a deal. But Xiong spends a couple of weeks in the Valley every year, looking for deals. He says Tencent's core strength is "patience."

And even if a deal doesn't happen? With only 20 percent of China's massive population currently online, Xiong is confident Tencent will eventually be the largest Internet company in the world anyway. Investors are confident, too. Tencent's price-to-earnings ratio at the time of publication was more than six times Google's, and the stock has appreciated faster than Apple's in recent years. It's easy to say Tencent is overvalued, but it's also clear that no other single Internet company is positioned to dominate the world's largest online market in the same way.

Here's the more amazing thing about Tencent: The core of its business is instant messaging—a product that AOL, Google, Yahoo!, Microsoft, and Facebook have never figured out how to monetize. Everyone calls Chinese search company Baidu the Google of China, but in a broader sense, Tencent is closer to pulling off the equivalent of what Google pulled off in the United States.

Before Google, search was seen as a necessary feature for any portal, but not a particularly desirable one. Search boxes sent users away from a site like Yahoo! or AOL. Those sites viewed themselves like a department store: they only made money if people stayed within their virtual walls. Back in the late 1990s, then Yahoo! CEO Tim Koogle used to brag in analyst meetings that clicks on searches were actually going *down*, because it meant fewer people were leaving the site.

The attitude toward IM has been much the same. It sucks up bandwidth and engineering time with little return. Ads never worked well, and it wasn't a tool that users would pay for with so many free options on the market. But Google turned search from a loss-leading feature into one of the world's largest Internet businesses, and Tencent did the same for instant messaging.

It wasn't easy. Tencent wasn't started by a polished executive who had spent time in the West like Robin Li of Baidu or Jack Ma of Alibaba Group. It was started by a young entrepreneur named Ma Huateng, nicknamed Pony Ma because "Ma" is Chinese for horse. Ma is written about daily in the Chinese press, but he almost never gives interviews. While most Internet companies team around Beijing and Shanghai, Tencent is down South with the factories in Shenzhen.

It's not about being the next Mark Zuckerberg; in China, the Web entrepreneur game is about being the next Pony Ma. Tencent's company store is called the Image Café, and it's a coded message: "I" is the same sound as the Chinese word for "love," "Ma" is Pony Ma's last name, and "Ge" means brother. *I love brother Pony.* The company has that familiar cocky edge of an Internet darling at its do-no-wrong moment in time. That kind of energy that you hate but also want to be part of. "*Don't hate us because we won! Join us!*" *Wink*

Ma wasn't quite so adored back in 2000. Tencent had ripped its IM service, QQ, off of Israel's ICQ and put it online as a free download. Millions of Chinese used it, but no one wanted to pay for it, and the online advertising market in China was nonexistent. Tencent had managed to find two investors to fund the company, but their $1.1 million investment was running low, and both investors were anxious to sell their shares and move out of the now-dodgy Web sector. The company was being shopped around for nearly any price to China's largest portals, but no one wanted to waste money on a company doing IM. Suddenly, revenue and profits—not users, hype, and promise—were all that mattered on the Web, and if the mighty AOL couldn't make money off IM, who could?

Like a lot of great Web entrepreneurs, Ma got lucky. China Mobile decided to share a portion of revenues with third-party companies that could help boost the number of people buying data plans. Ma thought quick chat-like messaging with friends—à la the pager—would be a hit on these phones. Finally, at a rate of six cents per month per user, Tencent started to make money. Ma augmented that income by using the service to push anything else a mobile user might pay for—ringtones, wall paper, horoscopes, and the like—all of the things that mobile phone companies in the United States would discover they could charge for years later.

In 2001, when Internet companies were crashing around the world, pennies over mobile phones were netting Tencent nearly $6 million per year in sales and a respectable $1.2 million in profits.[1] Ma started offering the same kinds of little virtual goods—avatars, outfits, pets—on the online product, and users paid up for them there, too. Tencent's audience was mostly only children, thanks to China's one-child policy, and the service just resonated with them. Growing up alone, many had active imaginary friends and imaginary worlds, so the idea of a virtual self wasn't creepy or nerdy, it was commonplace. And each only child had two parents and four grandparents filling their pockets with loose change every week. As these kids wiled away the hours at Internet cafés, Ma was one of the first to give them something to spend those pennies on.

As Ma was figuring all this out, Naspers, a media company out of South Africa, was smart enough to see where things were going. It spent some $30 million buying out Ma's earlier investors and enough founders' stock to own 50 percent of Tencent. That stake is now worth more than $20 billion, making it the most successful foreign investment in all of the Chinese Internet. And, amazingly, cash-generating Tencent never had to spend that money. It's still in the bank, Xiong says.

∞

Most Americans think they know two things about the Chinese Web: It's full of copycats and full of censorship. They're half right on both, but it's not nearly that simple. Let's deal with copycats first.

Product-wise, Tencent's QQ was so directly ripped off ICQ that the original name was "OICQ." When it lost a patent-infringement suit, it decided to change its name to the only somewhat less obvious QQ, and its own patents now hang framed in the headquarters office. But while chat may have been an old idea, in terms of monetization, Ma was five to ten years ahead of U.S. Web companies. He built chat not to be a productivity tool but to be a community for bored kids to hang out in online, sort of a pre-MySpace online mall. Friends were essentially staying in touch through 140-character bursts on phones over QQ, well before Twitter was created. Although U.S. companies are only now marveling at the idea of selling virtual goods for real cash, Tencent was doing that back in 2001.

If Tencent is a copycat, it has good company amid the U.S. Internet royalty: Google wasn't the first to do search; Facebook wasn't the first to do social networking; Microsoft ripped off much of Windows from Apple, which ripped it off of Xerox's Palo Alto Research Center; and the iPod was as late to the MP3 race as the iPhone was to the smartphone market. The first company to pioneer a market often fails but opens the door for future competitors.

Like startups during a recession, Chinese Web companies have benefited from building within constraints. Taobao, an online marketplace owned by Alibaba Group, won where eBay couldn't, because it created an elaborate network of bike couriers who could deliver goods and accept cash on delivery. eBay could work in the United States, because Americans had a history of buying things via catalogs and had a mature enough postal and banking system to make the transactions frictionless. eBay could just be a Web marketplace, but Taobao had to create a system by which it could work in China with huge challenges like China's fits and starts of modernity, geographic size, and disparity in quality of life.

Process and execution are vital to building a big Chinese company. Every element has to be thought through. And frequently, that's led to stronger, more defensible businesses, even on the Internet where the barriers to entry are notoriously low. Simply put, ideas are just that; execution is what matters. Sina may seem like a Yahoo! clone, Ctrip may seem like an Expedia clone, Taobao may seem like an eBay clone, and Baidu may seem like a Google clone, but each of these businesses have won in the battle for the massive Chinese Internet audience for a reason, and it wasn't that the government protected them. The Chinese government shuts down plenty of Chinese Web names that stray too, as the online video sites learned.

Most Chinese Internet companies win by innovating not around product, but like Tencent, around process and monetization. It's where the Chinese entrepreneur excels, which is interesting because it's where the typical Silicon Valley entrepreneur is the weakest. Like Roy Ho says about China's hardware wars, it's about staying in shape and running to the destination faster than the competitor.

⌒∞⌒

Song Li is one of the more unabashed Chinese entrepreneurs when it comes to copying Western ideas. He trolls Silicon Valley blogs every day looking for the hottest new company to rip off, only he doesn't call it ripping off, he calls it "innovation arbitrage."

Li invested in a job board called ChinaHR that was bought by Monster.com for $200 million, making him his first chunk of money. Then he founded a mobile version of an online dating site that he sold to Sina.com, one of China's largest portals. He was onto something, he thought. He started an incubator called SinoFriends that founded three ventures that Li alternates running. All are so-called innovation arbitrage plays off of Western ideas.

But just like the example of eBay and Taobao, the differences are pretty substantial. Li's current dating site, Zhenai, is practical, efficient, and brutally honest—much like China's no-nonsense customer base. With China's vast urban migration, loneliness and isolation are widespread emotions, and the pressure to find a mate before your late twenties is high. Chinese migrants work a minimum of 10 hours a day, so the more efficient way to meet that mate, the better. Nothing boosts efficiency like reducing something as mythic, romantic, fuzzy, and unquantifiable as love down to numbers and probabilities. There's no "you're-beautiful-on-the-inside" U.S.-style, feel-good message here. Modern China isn't about feelings; it's about results.

To get better results, Li scours his users' progress and mines it for data that he can turn into advice. For example, he's learned that 60 percent of women with long, straight hair get second dates—even when the data is normalized for Chinese women being more likely to have long, straight hair. The worst group is women with short, curly hair, who have just a 5 percent second-date percentage. Men also like black pantyhose and shiny, colorless nail polish, and they are universally attracted to women with a .7 hip-to-waist ratio—something Li believes is genetically hard-coded as a reproductive trait. "We're not telling them what to do, we're just giving them information," Li says matter-of-factly. "I can't do anything if a woman is fat, but I can tell her to dress so it shows off her waist." Song Li can find you a man—you just may have to wear a belt or grow your hair out first.

Women, on the other hand, prefer that their dates wear suits and are predisposed to look for "good providers." Li says he can track for every extra 1,000 RMB a man makes per month, statistically what percentage more attractive he will be to an average woman. "It's a math fact," he says. "I can build you a model."

This is an utterly Chinese approach. I was at a dinner one night when one woman asked a friend she hadn't seen for a while which of his kids his wife liked better. To my surprise, he answered, "I think she likes the older one."

"Is it because she's prettier?" the woman asked in all seriousness.

"No, it's because she's funnier," he answered.

(The younger one was a newborn baby.)

In modern China, getting a husband or finding a better job is about standing out. Standing out is about being better. You can make yourself better. Just like starting a business, it's about process and execution.

China has a long history of matchmaking, so just going online, finding someone you like, and messaging them isn't going to appeal to a lot of the population. The ones who are comfortable with doing that will just use social networks, and QQ's chat rooms are filled with people trolling for mates, or something less permanent. That's how Pony Ma met his wife, in fact. For the more traditional, there are already established offline alternatives in some 200,000 very local, fragmented matchmaking companies, charging anywhere between 2,000 and 60,000 RMB for a six-month contract. Even in comparatively cheap China, these companies have high customer acquisition costs because of their brick-and-mortar storefronts and heavy placements of classified advertising to keep recruiting new singles.

Li is seeking a middle ground: a Web site that's free to join and free to search, with revenues generated by a 350-person call center of matchmakers. Once you find someone you like on the site, you place a call to a matchmaker to set up a date. Using the service costs 3,000 RMB (roughly $430 in U.S. dollars) for a six-month subscription—about the same as the low end of a traditional matchmaking service but still high for an Internet subscription. The matchmaker determines whether both people want to go out, or suggests an alternative date from among the site's 22 million registered members, a number that's growing by about 40,000 members per day. The matchmaker then sets up the date and follows up afterward.

The matchmaker isn't your friend; she is doing a job. Her focus is on results, not feelings. Suggest someone out of your league, and she will guide your expectations lower. "We just want you to be realistic," Li says. And in the event of a rejection, she'll ask the rejecter to complete a detailed questionnaire to determine exactly why he or she didn't want another date. Then she'll call the other party to explain—in precise detail—where he or she went wrong. "At least you know why, and there are certain things you can fix next time," Li says.

Standing in an orange room full of 20-something matchmakers on headsets, Li and I eavesdrop on a random call.

"Our algorithm has found a few girls for you. The first one makes 3,000 RMB a month and you make 5,000 RMB per month. Is that going to be a problem?"

The guy says no.

"She has a very outgoing personality. Is that okay with you?"

The guy says it is, but apparently this point needed underlining, making me wonder if outgoing girls statistically don't get many second dates either. The operator emphasized, "She is the year of the Horse. She talks a lot. You are not going to be able to fix this about her."

That was okay, too.

"If there's anything you feel uncomfortable asking her, I can do it for you," the girl said as she took his payment information and scored a commission.

Just like the dating world in China, Zhenai is highly competitive. Arrange the most dates in a day and you win. If your team arranges the most dates, they win. And if the division—made up of smaller teams—arranges the most dates, it wins. Trophies are given out once a month. When I walked into the call center in the morning, teams were huddled around the room, breaking up with some sort of "let's go!" chant exclaimed in Chinese and running to the phones.

It may sound like labor-powered, innovation-free China, but it's not. Li has built a specific customer-management software system from scratch to walk matchmakers through the process, and he's hired a psychologist to help train them on what questions to ask and what to say to the lovelorn.

Li is hedging his bets with Zhenai—it's not an easy play in a market where most Internet users aren't used to paying more than ten cents for things online. He also has an application store—like the one for the iPhone—but for low-market phones, and he also has Digu, a company that changes what innovation it is arbitraging every time I see Li. First it was photo sharing. Then it was Twitter. Then it was a "location-based micro-blog with social gaming"— pretty much a mash-up of every buzzword in Silicon Valley at the time. His business card has Zhenai on one side and Digu on the other. Li is a junkie, and the Internet and China's huge, growing, consuming mass of users are his addiction.

His goal is to take each of the three companies public (one is not enough, he insists) and make enough money that he can get into the movie business. Only he doesn't want to invest in movies, the way some U.S. Internet moguls have. He wants to write and direct. He already took a screenwriting class and was frustrated at how much work it was. He's not sure he's good at it, so he hopes to make enough money from his Web ventures that even if no one comes to see his movies, his finances are assured.

Has he thought of ideas? Of course he has. This is Song Li—the man who believes everything fits into a framework, a preexisting template. The first movie will be about couples separated in the late 1940s, when Taiwan separated politically from the mainland. A lot of stories are told about separation, but most only tell the story from the side of the mainlanders. Like how Zhenhai expanded on Match.com, Song Li's version will up the ante by showing what happens on both the mainland and in Taiwan, following three couples. They'll all swap romantic partners along the way. If one couple is good, three is better, right?

Just like the Chinese economy is building several areas in parallel, so too do Chinese entrepreneurs tend to build companies in parallel. There's no value put on focus; the value is on land-grab. It's less "go big or go home" and more "grab this before someone else does."

In China, labor is the easy answer to any problem, and Li is amassing an army of smart Web wunderkinds. Every year he gives a talk to the local university's computer science grads, encouraging them to apply to work at his company. He gets thousands of applications and culls through them to find the 15 best ones. He puts them all in a room together—at the school, on the spot. He gives them 15 minutes to sketch out what Web site they would build if money weren't an issue. They then present the ideas, the group debates them, and then everyone votes. The kids think that the test is their idea winning, but it's not. Song Li is in another room watching all this, judging them on how they interact. He doesn't get all his picks—he's lucky to get even a few—but he wins enough to keep the innovation arbitrage engine running.

Ideas are just ideas. Process wins in China.

∞

China is perceived to be the most closed, censored, un-self-expressive country on the planet, and yet it is the only country outside of the United States that's given rise to several huge Internet companies worth billions of dollars. It's a paradox because people tend to think of the Internet as an inherently free and democratizing force. How do these two opposite approaches so profitably coexist in China, when they don't in huge democratic markets like India and Brazil?

One obvious difference is that the Chinese population has greater access to the Internet, which—love it or hate it—is the result of a central government that invests in building infrastructure for a "harmonious society." In exchange, the government expects that harmonious society to play by its rules. This is the case across the board in China. Right or wrong in terms of human rights, China has taken care of the basic needs of its emerging, chaotic, urbanizing migrating population with dignity compared to other developing countries. It is not a utopia, but you don't see anywhere near the slums like you see in India or the violence like you see in Brazil. And that, in part, has made the opportunity to build huge businesses in China greater.

Americans want to talk to Internet entrepreneurs who confess how oppressed they are over drinks and in hushed conversations, but the honest truth is that everyday Chinese people complain about their situation less than people in any country I've been to.

This isn't out of fear; many Chinese entrepreneurs I've met are una-bashed capitalists, have spent time in the West, and are hopeful that the country will move to democracy at some point. They are openly critical of the government and Chairman Mao. I've met half a dozen who were in Tiananmen Square in 1989 and fled to the United States afterward, thinking they'd never return home.

But most of these entrepreneurs say that China is freer today than it has ever been. It may be two steps forward and one step back, but that's still one step forward. Victor Ku of YouKu sees working with the government as his responsibility as an Internet CEO in a country growing and transforming this quickly. "We understand what is black and white and what is grey," he says. "We understand how to work with the government, and if we get it wrong we are just a phone call away. We have a consistent dialog."

Most Internet companies censor something, whether it's extreme hate speech, sexual content, copyrighted content, or in the case of eBay, auctions of Nazi memorabilia. The question is whether politi-cal criticism crosses a line. "Everyone has a different point of view," Ku says. "What about if we censored racy content? We wouldn't get criticized for that. We want to have a position of social influence. It's evolution here, not revolution."

Many Americans find this point of view horrific. Google specifically objected to the way the Chinese censor data, continu-ally changing the secretive list of things that are verboten and trolling the Web daily to have them removed. Many in the Valley cheered the search engine's 2010 decision to move from the main-land to Hong Kong. There's no way to whitewash the moral impli-cations: In 2005, Yahoo! got a human-rights black eye from its decision to turn over a blogger's identity to the Chinese government that wound up putting him in jail, and even homegrown Tencent has been criticized for turning over information on users when the government asks. But it's the cost of doing business in China.

For many Chinese, Ku makes a valid point. China doesn't have a national debt, and it still spends billions on an elaborate national infrastructure. While urbanization is rapid, taxing the roads and driving up the cost of living, China invests billions in building up satellite cities where people have equivalent—based on cost of living—economic opportunities to Shanghai or Beijing, and it's building high-speed trains to connect these places more easily. Since the 1970s, China's growth of 9.7 percent per year has lifted several hundred million people out of poverty, according to the World Bank. China alone is responsible for 75 percent of the poverty reduction in the emerging world over the last two decades. You may not want to live in a dorm of a manufacturing company, but having seen the living conditions there and slums in India and Brazil, I'd take the dorm.

What is happening in China has never happened in the world before, and China is handling its chaotic growth and massive economic and structural changes as well as any government could be expected to. The view from most entrepreneurs I've spoken with—even those who moved to China from the United States—is: "Democracy is important, but it's a luxury. We'll take successful capitalism first." Says Roy Ho, the Shenzhen mobile phone billionaire, "Deng Xiaoping has been the difference between what we have today in China and what they have in North Korea." Ho was in Tiananmen Square. He saw horrible things. Even still, sitting in a Pizza Hut in Shenzhen a few blocks from the $1-billion-dollar company he started a few years ago from scratch, he says he's grateful to Deng.

The question is what happens when that surging economy stumbles. That fear is the biggest reason the central government says it still needs control over its people. It's exerting less outwardly oppressive mind control and more a steady campaign of soft power. It's less about banning pictures of Tiananmen Square and more about preventing too much of an embrace of the Western ways so that another Tiananmen doesn't occur.

We've already been seeing fragments of the government's fear becoming reality with the strikes by factory workers that have roiled smaller cities since the late 2000s. Given that 400 million people get their information and entertainment online in China, the Web will continue to play a central role. The Web generation will, too. Throughout China, young urban professionals say that when their generation is in power, things will evolve. "I believe every country has the generation that makes the greatest contribution to what that country is going to become," said one young urban professional in Suzhou. "We are that generation. I have friends who felt their whole life they would not come back to China; they felt this acutely and now they are coming back."

The U.S. Ivy League kids flocking to Beijing may call themselves America's Lost Generation, but their Chinese counterparts flocking to the same cities for the same opportunities consider themselves China's Greatest Generation. The haunting question is what that generation stands for, other than money and things. The Chinese have never been a particularly religious culture, and the oppressiveness of the communist government stamped out any sense of morality except that which you could find in Chairman Mao's little red book. Loyalty to the party was the core of life down to the most obedient peasants in society—it trumped religion, nationalism, learning, and art. As communism loosens its grasp on China, holes are being punched in that core, mostly in the name of technology, consumerism, and capitalism.

In 2010, there was a particular concern about a wave of popular TV dating shows in China. They all follow the same formula: a stage full of girls cruelly asking questions of a would-be suitor, saying things like "If you don't drive a BMW, don't even think about it," or "You are so ugly, why are you here?" The girls take themselves out of the running, round after round, by turning off their lights. At the end, the poor guy finally gets to make a choice out of the ones still illuminated.

These shows are a powerful outlet for a wave of young, educated, financially self-sufficient women who came into the workforce as China was opening up its economy and who have decided not to marry simply for the sake of security or tradition. This group had been teased in society and called The Left Behinds, and these game shows were their way of reclaiming their independence. But to older generations, they also reveal a vapid society that praises money and things over traditional Chinese values of family and home.

Ironically, capitalism is the closest thing there is to a core in so-called communist China these days. As long as the country is still growing and lives are improving, economic progress is the glue holding the harmonious society together.

But your typical Web entrepreneur in China doesn't have time to worry about these bigger questions. His world is spinning too fast. Changes in regulations can pop up momentarily, putting him out of business overnight. In the lateral land-grab of opportunity, Tencent or Sina could jump into his business at any moment, demolishing his prospects with a flood of users that already out-number the population of the United States.

For foreign investors, betting on Web startups in China is an act of faith and playing the portfolio percentages. Some of the savviest investors have been lied to and cheated, and whole companies have disappeared overnight. They don't know what to do when it comes to normal ways of doing business in China, like paying bribes and closing deals at karaoke bars that are thinly veiled fronts for prostitution. There's a pulsating worry that all this money is being thrown down a black hole, and that they're the dumb American and the joke is on them. But despite all of these concerns, almost no one pulls out of the country; instead more money floods in. In the same quarter that Google pulled out of China, funding from U.S. venture capitalists increased 30 percent, and half a dozen Silicon Valley–based Web 2.0 companies opened offices there.

The lure of China, with the opportunity to fund the next Tencent, or worse, the fear of *missing* the next Tencent, is just too great. Just like for the wide-eyed Ivy League kids at the Drum and Bell Tower, China is the center of the high-risk, high-reward universe.

India

6

India's Invisible Infrastructure

*I*ndia is not comfortable, at all. Even in the most developed cities, the priciest hotels are usually surrounded by slums. Wafting through the air is the smell that results from so many people living with no running water, no electricity, and no sewage system. Out of 1.1 billion people, the World Bank estimates that just 33 percent of Indians have access to modern sanitation, and some 300 million live below the poverty line. In India, you never just happen upon a slum. You can always smell them coming. And yet, the sight of the slums is so much harder to take.

The traffic is the worst I've seen in any country. In China, drivers ignore speed limits and lanes, but they manage to move together like a school of fish, weaving in and out of each other's paths harmoniously. In India, driving is a zero-stakes game of survival for each patch of cracking asphalt between mopeds, rickshaws, cars, ramshackle trucks, grungy cows, mangy dogs, mud-caked pigs, and beggars who wander between cars, tapping on windows with hollow expressions, trinkets, and outstretched hands. Even if the traffic were light, drivers frequently don't know where to go because there's little urban planning and few street signs. It's this bad, and so far fewer than 5 percent of Indians have their own vehicles. On top of that, there are sewage backups, power outages, and other daily manifestations of an overtaxed, unplanned, outdated urban infrastructure.

India's tourism board spent millions on an award-winning ad campaign touting the country as "Incredible India!" But at first blush, it seems that nothing in India is as advertised. The realities of Indian life are shocking given the legacy of democracy and capitalism the Brits allegedly left in their imperialist wake, and the billions of dollars that have flooded into the country in recent years thanks to outsourcing. One of the country's biggest strengths is supposed to be its representative legal system. But while it might be a good system on paper, in reality it would take more than 300 years for the backlogged cases in Indian courts to be heard. That makes individual business relations a Wild West of bribes and intimidation. The World Bank ranks India among the 20 worst countries for setting up a business and next to last among 183 nations when it comes to the ease of enforcing contracts. In India, the words "I'll sue!" have been stripped of any meaning.

China is known for low-level sweatshop labor, whereas India is known for outsourced, white-collar jobs. India is supposed to be the highbrow intelligentsia of the developing world. So why are there rivers clogged with waste sludging through the middle of its most lucrative, developed white-collar cities? When Chinese businesspeople argue that democracy can't work in a country of

1 billion people and an American counters, "What about India?" The typical response you get in China is: "Exactly."

It's hard to square this India—the one that pummels your senses at every step—with the India that millionaire Silicon Valley executives say is getting so much better every year, and the U.S. government insists is the next great superpower to counterbalance China. Indian nationals who return to India say they can't believe the country's progress, but they typically move into cloistered, gated communities with a staff of live-in servants who do the shopping, run the errands, and pick up the kids. Groceries? Yoga Masters? Masseuses? They all come to them.

Naren Bakshi founded Versata, an enterprise software company in the Valley that he took public in the late 1990s. He also cofounded TiE, an Indian entrepreneur networking organization that started in the Valley and has branches around the world. He moved back to his hometown of Jaipur and has a stunning 10,000-square-foot home with the finest marble floors, a balcony off every bedroom, and an entire floor he uses just for parties. A Vonage phone line rings when someone calls his Silicon Valley number—just like he never left. A German machine washes and rewashes and washes again the lettuce and fruit they buy, because his wife—who is also from India—is paranoid of the dreaded "Delhi belly."

"The livability inside the house is good; it's the same as our house in Fremont [California]," Bakshi says. "The problem is we can't control the outside of the home." So he's just trying to expand the area he can control. He's already convinced the neighbors to clean and gate the community and keep it clean. Bakshi is trying to reclaim and fix his India, one square meter at a time.

There's a confused reality here. If India is getting so much better, why do Indians who return home hide from the everyday life of it? And if India isn't getting better, why go back home? There are a few answers I've gotten to these questions. The first is that things were that much worse, 10 to 20 years ago. "Sure, the unhygienic conditions mean people get sick, but now if someone is sick, they can get medical treatment," said Manoj Tiwari, matter-of-factly. "Before they used to die."

The statistics support that gradual improvement. India is changing, just very slowly. Across averages like poverty rate, literacy, or life expectancy, the average improvement in quality of life in India is roughly 1 percent per year.[1] It may seem like watching grass grow, particularly compared with how quickly Israel created a high-tech ecosystem out of nothing and how quickly China lifted hundreds of millions of people out of poverty, but the grass *is* growing.

Indians are also incredibly nationalistic, and part of the insistence that things are getting better is pride, salesmanship, and wishful thinking. India is a nation of expression, vibrant color, and noise. The trucks you see clogging India's urban streets are decked out with bright colors, tiger-like eyes are painted around the headlights and feathers, ribbons, and pom-poms festoon the inside of the windshields. Women dress in saffron, fuchsia, and tangerine saris with arms full of gold and silver bangles. On every truck "HORN PLEASE" is painted across the bumper in bright letters—a message to smaller cars and mopeds that if the truckers can't hear them, they won't know they are there. Particularly in the north of the country, Indian culture is about leaning on that horn. "WE'RE HERE! WE'RE A SUPERPOWER! LOOK AT US!"

To be fair, the United States wanted India to be an instant superpower just as badly. In March 2005, a spokesperson for President George W. Bush's administration said the United States aimed "to help India become a major world power in the 21st century." Around the same time, a CIA report referred to India as the "swing state" in 21st-century global politics. Elsewhere, the United States referred to India repeatedly as a "natural ally."[2] There's obvious subtext here: China. There was a realization that India and China—by sheer population alone—were increasingly becoming forces on the world stage, and if the United States had to pick one, it was picking the democracy that spoke English as the lingua franca.

Silicon Valley doesn't always move in lockstep with the federal government, but in this case it wanted India to be the next great high-tech superpower as well. No ethnic group has been as success-ful in the Valley as Indians. Indians have founded more U.S. tech-nology companies in the last decade than immigrants from Britain, China, Taiwan, and Japan combined. More than one-quarter of all immigrant-funded tech companies over the last decade had an Indian founder.[3] But these statistics don't come close to sum-ming up the influence Indians have had on the buildout of Silicon Valley's glory years.

Aside from Vinod Khosla, co-founder of Sun Microsystems and one of the most famous venture capitalists in the world, most Indian entrepreneurs aren't household names, because they aren't known for inventing sexy consumer Internet companies. But when it comes to chips, routers, software and computer companies, no other group in Silicon Valley has been so successful at so many dif-ferent levels. Indians make up a lot of the Valley's gatekeepers, work-horses, and its high-tech elite, and that hasn't been handed to them. Most of them came to the Valley with nothing, and they earned the Valley establishment's money, respect, and, in many cases, awe.

So it was natural to think India could be the next great power-house for entrepreneurship and returns. The promise of India was to be an Israel with scale, an Israel with a huge domestic market, an Israel on steroids. Venture capital and private equity poured into India in the late 1990s, as everyone expected the Web would explode all over the subcontinent. PricewaterhouseCoopers flew around the country's major cities calling on any entrepreneurs that had a remotely interesting Web idea and telling them to tear up all their logical business plans and build something big—something that would attract eyeballs—all funded with U.S. money. They explained venture capital to a naïve 19-year-old Vishal Gondal of Indiagames as: "It's like taking money from a bank you don't have to pay back." Great, he said, with no idea of the downsides, where do I sign?

In Mumbai, Pravin Gandhi decided to try his hand at venture capital after he sold his company to Digital Equipment Corporation. It was shockingly easy to raise money back then. "I didn't realize it only took a dinner to get a million-dollar check," the crotchety, diminutive 70-year-old told me, sitting in the lush lobby of the Trident Hotel in South Mumbai. He raised a $35 million fund "with no clue how to be a venture capitalist."

Gandhi invested in Indiabulls and Indiagames, two of the few companies funded amid this mania that are still in business. These two deals ensured he had an internal rate of return of 17 percent on the fund, making it one of the best funds of the era, especially for India. But when the Internet bubble burst, Gandhi began to dread trips to meet with his U.S. limited partners, who were mostly Indian nationals. "Just as the money came easily in the 1990s, now the advice came easily," he says. "All these bitchers and moaners would show up, and I would tell them: You just have to wait." Gandhi is still investing in India, but now he invests in smaller, seed-fund amounts so he doesn't have to deal with so many fair-weather limited partners who expect Indian business to move at the speed of Silicon Valley.

Gandhi has a strange but common mix of being bullish on India in the long-term but critical of what he sees now. More than 10 years later, those early promises of India—especially its Web sector—still haven't proven true, he says. Gandhi criticizes Indians for being too content, too afraid to fail, and too quick to go for easy services revenues rather than try to build a great product or a great company. "People in Silicon Valley were led to believe India was the next great superpower," he says. "Bullshit superpower. We're not a superpower, we're service providers. Sometimes you tell yourself a lie so many times you start to believe it."

Why did the United States expect India to take off so fast? In short, because China did, because Indian entrepreneurs did so astoundingly well in the United States, and because multinationals found so much great outsourcing talent in India. Why didn't it take off? Part of it is India's democracy. Things just don't get done quickly in a democracy serving more than 1 billion people who don't speak the same language, don't have jobs, and don't have access to basic communications and infrastructure. And part of it is the nature of India. Before colonial times, India had never been a united country. During the struggle for independence, the founding fathers of India like Mahatma Gandhi and Jawaharlal Nehru ultimately failed to keep the country united, with Pakistan being carved off as a Muslim state. Gandhi and Nehru refused to give into India's Hindu majority, insisting that India—unlike Pakistan—remain a secular nation.

That didn't mean the country had no religion, but rather that none was above the others. The country bent so far to protect religious, linguistic, and territorial differences that unity was a challenge for most of its modern history. Fifty years of nearly endless territorial skirmishes and independence movements later, India has done what no pundit thought it could: The country has held together. But rather than the modern, English-speaking superpower everyone wanted India to become, India is a fragmented, polarized nation bickering in thousands of different tongues.

Naren Gupta, an Indian venture capitalist based in Silicon Valley, grants all of the empirical shortcomings of modern India, but he argues that the country grows on you. "Most people I know who do business in India hate it on their first trip, but if they go back, they wind up loving it," he says. Gupta's theory is that the visceral, sensory shocks are so extreme that you can't see anything beyond the chaos at first. Compare that to China, which is stunning in its efficiency and modernization. It's only when you return to India—albeit prepared for the worst—that you start to see the beauty and promise of the country, Gupta argues. That's what happened to him when he was deciding whether to invest in his homeland or not, and that's exactly what happened to me.

India *is* incredible. But paradoxically for a country that is so known for color and sound and spice, it's the things you can't see that bode well for the country's entrepreneurial future. The physical infrastructure is horrific, but India's invisible infrastructure is promising. If you can get past the barrage of cows and mopeds and poverty and power outages, there is a superpower in the making, but it's not happening quickly. And it's not because of India's democracy; it's largely despite it. There are four pillars of this invisible infrastructure where India has excelled: connections, education, telecom, and its services economy. This chapter will take a close look at the good and bad of each sector.

⚬❈⚬

Connections

As discussed already, Indians have dominated Silicon Valley's tech industry in a way almost no other ethnic group has. Part of the reason it accelerated in the late 1990s was because Indians learned to use their immigrant network so effectively. TiE, the group co-founded by Bakshi back in 1992, is the most tangible example.

TiE was started by a small group of Indian immigrants who had made it in the Valley and wanted to help others. The idea was drawing on the Indian tradition of gurus and disciples. The membership fit into one of the two categories: Gurus had to give their time and a minimum of $1,500 per year to the organization, and disciples were expected to become gurus when they achieved success.

Early on, TiE was focused on technology and Silicon Valley, and it's not difficult to find people who tell stories about getting nowhere until a TiE member funded them or made crucial introductions. But more quantifiable are the statistics that showed the rise of Indian entrepreneurs as TiE grew: In 1980 to 1988, only 7 percent of companies in the Silicon Valley were started by Indians. From 1995 to 2005, that number more than doubled to 15.5 percent, despite only 6 percent of the Valley population being Indian born.[4] The companies still had to perform on their own merit, but that network was giving them the opportunity to prove they could.

TiE members have been so successful that the biggest complaint about TiE today is that it's too much about self-interested networking among the elites and not enough about uplift. Still, flawed as it may be, TiE represents the powerful connection that exists between an Indian immigrant who has done well in the United States and Indians who are still struggling, whether in the United States or in India.

Aside from TiE, plenty of individual Indian successes feel the same pressure to give back. Some people describe it as guilt— the people who left India for a better life in the 1980s and 1990s feel badly about the family members and friends they left behind, especially considering the struggle for day-to-day life that still goes on in much of the country.

But whatever the reason, it's different from China's "Confucian bubbles" that contain just close friends and business partners moving around the world like colliding billiard balls. Indians seem more like that all-for-one, big, noisy family that fights all the time but also would do anything for each other. Unlike Israel and China, a lot of the money that's been invested in India hasn't made returns yet, but more keeps pouring in. In the first quarter of 2010, U.S. venture capital investments in India more than doubled to $259 million. The connection amid the Indian diaspora is a huge reason why. As a whole, the country's entrepreneurs keep getting second chances that many others wouldn't.

Education

I was in the slum for only a matter of moments before two smiling kids adopted me as their official American guest. "Come with me! I'll take you! I live there!" a small boy with a blue shirt and a perfect toothy grin said in Hindi as he ran ahead of me. His quiet friend in yellow jogged beside him smiling shyly, his jet-black Elvis curl bobbing on his forehead. These kids may have been born in a slum, but they had two things going for them: a cell phone in each of their pockets and a rickety computer terminal by the side of a road.

We meandered through the twisting streets deeper and deeper into the Delhi slum. The kids were trotting excitedly, smacking a cow on the rump, bragging about their tour guide role to a friend, hopping over a pile of trash in the street. At one point they got sidelined playing in a clump of unruly trees. The boy in blue, who did all the talking, pointed to the trees, looked at me, and carefully said in English, "jungle."

But we had a destination in mind: a row of computers set into a kiosk by the side of the road. These two boys had spent the last five years whiling away free hours there, playing games and learning English, math, and science. The boy in blue had learned computers from his older brother and liked to show off. He told me in Hindi when we first met: "I know computers *quite well.*"

This wasn't an empty boast. The boy in blue had figured out shortcuts in the games that the company that made the computers didn't even realize were there. A pecking order of older, bigger boys gathered around him as he tapped away. There was a sense of respect he might not have gotten on a slum street without a computer. He got absorbed in one game, and I asked what he was doing. He glanced over his shoulder and said nonchalantly, "science."

The so-called Hole-in-the-Wall computer program was started back in 1999 by Sugata Mitra, chief scientist of for-profit education company NIIT. At this time, most computer "labs" in Indian schools were made up of one or two computers used only under the strict supervision of a teacher. As a result, many kids only got to look at computers from across the classroom. But watching how quickly his son could pick up and navigate a cell phone, Mitra wondered what would happen if he left a computer out in the open for a group of children to discover. He had a hunch they didn't need instruction or supervision after all. There was a slum next to his office, so he knocked a hole in the wall and shoved a computer through it. He set up a camera on a tree limb to record what happened.

A 13-year-old, illiterate kid who'd never seen a computer before wandered over tentatively. Soon, he realized he could move the cursor by moving a finger across the touchpad. Within four hours, a small group of kids had gathered. They had figured out how to open Internet Explorer and were playing a game on Disney's Web site. "All of us were absolutely shocked watching that," says Abhishek Gupta, who heads the program now. Some of the team expected the kids to break or even try to steal the computer.

A pilot project with the World Bank followed, and NIIT set up 22 of these Hole-in-the-Wall kiosks around the country from 2001 to 2005. The organization studied the results, and the most obvious takeaway was that kids left on their own learn computers. The project also helped develop team-building and social skills—with 200 kids sometimes huddled around one screen. Whether the computers lead to more general academic improvement was less clear, but in many cases performance was up measurably, Gupta says.

Interestingly, when that partnership was over, NIIT didn't take the project down the nonprofit route. It sells the machines for between $6,000 and $20,000 mostly to the government, which has installed 500 of them around India. The for-profit approach isn't because NIIT is adverse to donors' money—it's opening a new high-end university that is run as a nonprofit. But there are two ways that Indians look at education: There's the high-end ivory tower learning for learning's sake and the kind of education that gets you a better life and a better job.

For NIIT, running the program as a business ensures its survival, but beyond that there's the knowledge that people in India will go without shoes or food if it means they can learn. With the government not providing much of a safety net, it's the best hope everyone has. As a result, more than 70,000 for-profit schools have sprung up in India, charging fees as little as a few U.S. dollars per course. The point here isn't the quality of the education, which varies widely. It's a unique cultural Indian lust for practical, usable education. The dual economy between those who live on $2 per day and those who make $20,000 per year is so great, and without connections, education is the only way up.

Everyone in India knows the route to the best jobs is the India Institute of Technology (IIT) system, frequently called the MIT of India. The education is not nearly as good as an American Ivy League school, but what is impressive about IIT is the selection process. Every kid takes an entrance exam, and the score on that exam determines your future.[5] It doesn't matter who you are; if you score well, then you have your pick of IIT campuses, majors, and, after that, jobs. Parents know this, so kids study and prepare for this exam daily from an early age. Nothing is more important.

But not everyone will get into an IIT. And that's why the for-profit educational market is so robust. NIIT teaches everything from four-year degrees to basic office etiquette and Western hygiene. Even Indian companies invest heavily in educating their own workforces. Infosys spends a minimum of six months schooling each employee, and that's a huge reason why people want to work there: they know they'll emerge able to work for anyone.

There are two ways of looking at this mania for learning in India: The first is that it represents another failing on the part of the public sector and a huge burden for companies. But the silver lining is the culture that's intensified around learning, the same way Israelis developed an endemic culture around risk taking. Indians love to argue about everything, and a big reason why is that in India nothing is better than looking smart.

In any country there are always elites, adults, politicians who talk up the importance of education, but in India everyone wants it, thirsts for it, yearns for it in a way that I've never seen. Because the people have been so let down by the government and the desire is so great, there's a greenfield opportunity in for-profit, practical learning that could one day be the envy of the world. Maybe it's another generation away, but this thirst is how the grass could finally start growing faster in India.

Telecommunications

Not every slum has a Hole-in-the-Wall terminal, and given the lack of basic infrastructure in the country, it's unlikely that every slum ever will. But every slum kid has a cell phone. This may be the single most important thing that India has gotten right. In 2000, only 3 million Indians had mobile phones, but by 2005, more than 100 million Indians did. By 2010, India had more than 500 million mobile phones and was registering some 20 million new phone numbers *per month*. For slow-growing India, where only 40 million people are on the Web, that's an explosion of progress.

Other than the railroad built out by the British, nothing else connects this disparate, sprawling, heat-scorched, and rain-pounded land. English is as close as the country comes to a lingua franca, but it's hardly universally spoken. Fewer than 10 percent of the country has access to the Internet, but roughly half of Indians—even those who labor in the cities making less than $2 per day—have a cell phone. But more impressive than the physical connectivity is the way telecom has been rolled out. The business model and low-cost approach is what has made the adoption so wide and the impact so much greater than any other technology to enter the country.

Indian service providers like Airtel and Reliance built out networks on the cheap by renting the towers and base stations from equipment providers like Nokia and Ericsson, until they had enough customers to buy the assets outright. "They turned capital expenses into operating expenses," says Sanjay Nayak, a Silicon Valley returnee who is building Tejas Networks, a telecom equipment company in Bangalore. Chinese Cisco competitor Huawei has done its part too, using its state-backed financial muscle to provide low-cost telecom equipment to the emerging world that a lot of Western companies can't match. And in India, 80 percent of the phones are prepaid. That's the best kind of customer, because they get their money upfront.

The result has been staggering: The cost of calls is down to a fraction of a penny per second, as these companies have found a way to make money charging users an average of $6 per month. In the United States, carriers need an average revenue of $50 per user per month to make money. There is also the phenomenon of the missed call. Many Indian cell phone plans only charge when someone makes a call and the person he or she is calling picks up. Some plans even charge a single upfront fee for lifetime connectivity, assuming you only receive calls. That means India's servants can receive calls from their employers without paying a single rupee, and they can even call their bosses, hang up, and wait for the bosses to call them back for free, too.

This is key to how India's urban dual economy functions. A small base of employers who can afford to make calls effectively subsidizes a massive base of service staff who can't afford it but have no other way to be connected. Being poor in India isn't about money. It's about having no permanence, identity, and living off the grid. The cell phone is the lifeline, in the same way that education is the way out and connections are the way up.

Telecom is the greenfield opportunity India got right, and that's mostly because of a few scrappy private companies, not the government. There is concern about the proliferation of towers dotting the cityscapes, but those are problems to solve later. For now, telecom has done what Nehru barely could: It has united India into one common system of SMS, sent, missed, and received calls that spans huge gulfs in language, literacy, religion, geography, and class.

The Service Economy

Another huge part of India's invisible infrastructure is its services industry—the only area where the country has excelled on a global business level, save perhaps Bollywood. A funny thing happened on the way to would-be modernity: India decided to skip its manufacturing phase and go straight from the farm to services. While more than 100 million people work in manufacturing in China, only 7 million Indians have jobs in the formal manufacturing sector.[6] Two-thirds still work on farms, and a small very lucky group gets to work in services.

The services industry includes all those things that the West outsources to India, such as writing software and answering calls from customers. Unlike China, India's 21st-century rise has largely been built on things you can't see, and the headquarters of much of this was Bangalore, in low-key Southern India. But not everyone agrees that this pillar of India's invisible infrastructure is a healthy one.

In one respect, no one has played the West's outsourcing revolution better than India. Its winners were able to skip the grueling factory jobs of China to go straight to high-paying—if dull—office jobs. Part of this was because Indians had the advantage of speaking English, at least in the top tiers of society. And thanks to the grueling life of trying to get into an IIT, many Indians have an amazing work ethic that's a boon when it comes to the drudgery of writing a lot of code. When it comes to call centers, Indians excel at telling people what they want to hear. Anyone who has been in the country has seen the head nod: It's as if Indians are tracing a tiny figure eight in the air with their noses. And when they do it, which is always, there's no way to tell if they're saying yes or no. Perhaps it goes back to colonial days, but whatever it is, confusion through effusive politeness is an Indian skill that long predates call center scripts.

There was a lot of bragging in the mid-2000s that India had cleverly skipped the manual part of modernization and joined the United States as a services economy of knowledge workers—in the same way that India as a nation had skipped the authoritarian dictatorships that plagued much of the developing world after colonization and gone straight to democracy. The services business is the one thing India has that the rest of the emerging world envies.

Second-tier cities in China are trying to replicate it, as are smaller nations in Latin America and Africa.

But there's a problem. Remember the production pyramid that has brand at the top, supported by design, engineering, and manufacturing? If Americans reap the most money at the top with brand, and Chinese get the benefits of mass employment from the base, Indians are somewhere in an uncomfortable middle. Engineering doesn't allow nearly as many people to benefit from the economic uplift of outsourcing, but at the same time most of the value from these jobs are going to the Western companies doing the outsourcing.

While many Indian techies are indeed doing more high-level service jobs, they're still doing them on the cheap for Western companies, and that means the bulk of the value of that knowledge, innovation, and work is not staying in India; it is flowing back to the United States. Is that the case in a greater degree with Chinese manufacturing? Yes, but China has been leveraging that expertise to create more of its own billion-dollar companies, like BYD and CK Telecom, that are climbing that stack. Meanwhile, China's superior infrastructure has allowed companies like Tencent and Giant to become mass new-media properties.

In China, manufacturing has been an important bridge for agrarian migrants, and thanks to dorms and cafeterias, it provides a social safety net that India's urban migrants lack. In China, the bulk of the social and economic progress has been in low-level factory jobs, but hundreds of millions are taking part in the move. In India, the recipients of modernization make more, but there are far fewer of them. While only 14 million people—out of 1.1 billion Indians—work in the formal private sector, fewer than 1 million work in information technology, call centers, and other back-office outsourced jobs. "India finds itself higher up the ladder than one would expect it to be. It is just that most of its people are still sitting at the bottom," writes author Edward Luce.[7]

Increasingly, cockiness at skipping the manufacturing economy drudgery is giving way to a concern that India needs to *make something.* "The services industry has had a phenomenal run, but we need to stop doing business for everyone else," says Nayak of Tejas Networks, one of the few companies in Bangalore that makes a product. "This is not scalable."

The implications of what Nayak is talking about can be seen throughout Bangalore. It's a fast-money scene of people who have skipped a major economic step. Kids out of college have suddenly graduated into a world where their entry-level salaries are substantially more than anyone in their families has ever made. Not only does it give them the freedom to move out of the joint-family home—where many generations share the same space and meddle in one another's lives—but it also gives them the freedom to buy an iPhone, an expensive watch, a nice car, and a Zippo lighter. Bangalore is the quintessential Indian expression of superficial modernity. U.S. brands and conspicuous consumption abound. Yet, much of the city still doesn't have the infrastructure basics like water, sewage, and power.

The would-be entrepreneur scene in Bangalore is much the same. There's glamour to being an entrepreneur in Bangalore, and there are certainly some legit players like Tejas and others. But I was repeatedly pitched by kids in their twenties and thirties who saved up money, quit their job at a multinational, and said that if their Silicon-Valley-cloned Web company didn't take off in a year they could always go back to another multinational. Meanwhile, entrepreneurs trying to build a company for the long haul frequently complain that Bangalore coders will only join for multinational-sized salaries, because compensation in the form of stock options carries little cultural weight.

This Bangalore isn't a new Silicon Valley. Silicon Valley is about taking risk, not eschewing it. It's about the long haul, not the quick flip, particularly when there's no evidence that Web companies in Bangalore can be flipped. This is play-acting, not entrepreneurship. "No one from call centers is starting companies," says Naren Gupta of Nexus Ventures, the investor who talked about how much better

India gets on a second visit. His firm's offices are in Mumbai and Delhi, not Bangalore, for this same reason. "The software talent is good in Bangalore, but they all want to sell," he says. "On the other hand, Bombay has a product culture, and Delhi is more aggressive and ambitious than either."

The story of Bangalore is the story of a large number of people comfortably leapfrogging into the middle class. There's nothing wrong with that, but many are not looking to take risk, they are looking for security, says Pankaj Chandra, the head of Indian Institute of Management in Bangalore. Chandra references a word you hear a lot in India—*Jugaad*. It means creatively finding a solution to something, frequently in a hacked-together, gerrymandered way. Jugaad is deep within Indian culture, as innovative solutions to core infrastructure problems can be found throughout slums and villages. But this approach rarely turns into scalable businesses. "We are great at Jugaad, but poor at systemizing it," Chandra says. "Indian entrepreneurship at its core is creative but not disciplined."

At its best, Jugaad is raw Indian creativity with little discipline, and Bangalore's army of service providers are the opposite. They are all discipline, no creativity, Chandra says. The constant repetition of giving life to another person's innovation has squeezed the Jugaad out of them. His words rang in my head when I went to a Bangalore Startup Saturday meet-up, where would-be entrepreneurs pitch ideas. The auditorium was filled with Banglore's IT army: men in their mid-thirties with closely groomed moustaches, dressed in starched-blue, tucked-in, button-up shirts and jeans. It is a different world from the fire, chaos, and creativity that defines India for better or for worse. "It's fallen out of the system," Chandra says. "The IT manager has lost all creativity. I'd like to think in fifty years IT has lead to so much entrepreneurship. But most follow the secure path. It's the ones who aren't from elite institutions—the ones from tougher backgrounds that are bright enough to make a difference—those are the ones who are changing India."

Many Indians argue the problem with local entrepreneurship is that Indians become easily contented. Part of this is rooted in the dominant religion of the country, Hinduism. Hinduism teaches tolerance and temperance and contentment. Unlike Protestantism, there's no implicit benefit to greed and hard work. I mentioned to a crowd of Indian students that Israelis made great entrepreneurs because they lived like there was no tomorrow. One smart student responded, "We live like we have infinite lifetimes, what does that mean for us?" It means Indians move slowly, plan, and as a culture, live without urgency. "People are too accepting of all the infrastructure problems, so everything in India moves in slow motion," Naren Gupta says. The big challenge for Bangalore is fighting that contentment. It's a place that suddenly has something to lose—compared to the India all around them, *a lot* to lose.

If you buy that the hugely successful services business has strangled Indian Jugaad in the name of comfortable middle-class lives, there's one man who is disproportionately responsible for a lot of this attitude: Narayana Murthy. Murthy is the founder of Infosys, the first Indian company to go public on the NASDAQ and the company that kicked off the $30 billion IT outsourcing revolution that has changed Indian lives and enraged out-of-work Americans.

Long before Murthy was one of the most famous capitalists in India, he was a kid wrapped up in India's Nehru-lead love affair with socialism. He went to France in the 1970s to learn more about the then-raging communist movement, as did a young Deng Xiaoping. Murthy was convinced that some form of communism or socialism was the only way to solve India's poverty problem. Murthy was 26 years old, and after 11 months on the road he was hitchhiking through Eastern Europe back home to India to spread the good, Red word.

Murthy got dropped off at a train station somewhere near the Yugoslavian border. He was hungry, and the station's restaurant was closed, so he settled in and waited nearly 12 hours for it to open. When morning came, he realized the restaurant only took Yugoslavian dollars, which he didn't have. This was before ATMs and credit cards, so Murthy went into town, but it was Sunday in a communist country and no one was working. He hiked back to the station, his stomach now burning with hunger. He lay down to sleep on the platform until his train came—the best way to conserve calories, he figured.

Finally, the train came, and Murthy was on his way. He was seated in a compartment with a young couple, and he was chatting up the girl in French. The boy, who didn't speak French, got angry at Murthy and stormed off. The next thing Murthy knew, Yugoslavian policemen were pulling him off the train and throwing him into an eight-foot-by-eight-foot concrete cell. They confiscated his passport, sleeping bag, and backpack, and he was held for 72 hours. He was never given a reason and, adding to his misery, he still hadn't eaten.

After three days, the door opened without explanation, and Murthy was dragged by the guards and thrown into a freight car with a busted window. He was told he would be free when he reached Istanbul, which meant 21 more hours without food. As snow pelted him through the busted glass, the only thing Murthy could feel for those 21 hours was blinding rage. These five days of misery had been his painful education on what communism was really about. By the time he got back in India, he was done with the idea that it protected the little guy. A newly avowed capitalist, Murthy and some friends started Infosys years later, a company that makes more than $4 billion per year writing software for other companies at reliable quality and a lower price. He's now helped create hundreds of dollar-millionaires in India and many more rupee-millionaires. Murthy was the CEO for 21 years, but he's stepped back now, mostly serving as a statesman for the company, and frequently, India's service sector in general.

At the time, most entrepreneurs in India were small mom-and-pop textile makers, traders, and jewelers, or wealthy industrialists made rich with government monopolies, contracts, and favors. As assets, Murthy seized on India's intangibles, the invisible infrastructure of networks, a work ethic, and a desire to learn. "India missed the industrial revolution, but Indians had intelligence," he says. "We had to make do with pen and paper. We were always forced to look at the abstract."

As much as Infosys is loved by Indians, companies like it are hated by Americans who blame all that cheap, willing labor for the U.S. jobs that have gone overseas. Murthy responds to such critics with a global view. He says that he has a GE fridge, drove a Ford to work for many years, uses a Dell Laptop, and drinks Coca-Cola. India used to make competing products, but the U.S. versions were better, and when India became less protectionist, the better products won. That put millions of Indians out of work, Murthy argues, but cheaper products with better distribution made life for hundreds of millions more Indian consumers better. Similarly, Murthy says that cheaper, better software and services makes U.S. multinationals stronger. It's hardly his fault if those savings flow back to shareholders or CEO bonuses and not into higher-level local jobs or job training.

Murthy shrugs off worries that India is too reliant on services. He says, "The first stage of any economy is creating jobs. Then people can start spending. What is happening in India today is the creation of jobs. Let's create jobs any way we can as long as it's legal and ethical. It doesn't matter what it is as long as it makes money and satisfies customers. There will come the opportunity for making products."

Nayarana Murthy hasn't created a product company, but he's created billions in market value for investors and a new natural resource for India—cheap reliable coders that his company spends months training and that the best multinationals compete to hire. He says he doesn't know if India will ever look like the United States or China, but he has a greater confidence in the younger generation of Indians than he had in his own.

Even the naysayers don't go so far as to say Infosys—and its services revolution—haven't been on balance a huge positive for the country. The question is whether that surge in quality of life can spread to more than 1 percent of the population. The answer, as always with India, is in the slums and the villages, and the huge economy found there that's built on all things tiny.

7

India's Mighty Microeconomy

*W*ith fewer than 1 percent of Indians living the high-paid services dream, building a big consumer company in India isn't easy. How do you reach a fragmented, poor market? Think small and talk to someone like Lakhan Lal.

It's not hard to find him—or hundreds of thousands like him—throughout India. He's everywhere from the busy street corner in the largest city to the side of the road in the most remote village. A guy like Lal sells the most in those grungy urban neighborhoods that Indians describe as places where "you can't tell if the sewer drain is in the street or the street is in the sewer drain."

Lal is a man of few words, which may have something to do with the constant flow of traffic coming in and out of his shop. It would need a revolving door if it had a door at all. As is, the shop's facade is either wide open for business or locked tight by a pull-down garage door. That door protects a mini-empire. In a working-class Delhi neighborhood where migrant workers earn less than 3,000 rupees a month doing everything from delivering food to building the new airport, Lal's tiny shop has huge traffic. And all those people come there every day to buy tiny things: mobile airtime by the second, one pill, a day's worth of shampoo.

Some of the things Lal sells, like mobile minutes, require a passport photo in India, nevermind that most Indians never leave their cities, much less the country. No problem: Lal has a blue backdrop on the wall and a digital camera. He pulls it out—with a totally deadpan face—and snaps a photo of me as I'm asking him questions. I'm not sure if this is defensive or mischievous, but the picture can't be pretty. It's a hot, sticky day, I've been vomiting for 48 hours, and we're only standing a few feet from each other. There's little room in the store for much beyond the counter that Lal is crowded behind with a sulky-looking teen who is blaring a Bollywood video on YouTube, playing on the Acer computer that catalogs Lal's microworld. It's a cheap computer, but it's likely the most expensive thing in the store. Lal seems to know everyone who comes in and what they want the second he sees them. A customer barely leans in the store, mutters a word or two in Hindi, plunks down a few rupees, and Lal tosses the customer the desired, tiny treasure.

Before independence, India was a feudal society made up of hundreds of kingdoms and princes. Today in places that live paycheck to tip to handout, people are still focused around one, central person who provides just enough for them to make it. The prince has given way to the corner grocer. And in modern India, that thing Lal's customers are coming here to buy is almost always something that costs just a few rupees and fits in the palm of his or her hand.

Over the course of a month, Lal makes thousands of rupees per item. A big seller is Pantene, which offers "sachets" of shampoo and conditioner, just enough for a day's use and typically reserved for a special occasion. Strings of these sachets are hung on wires in every cornerstore and ramshackle kiosk in the country, looking like condoms or packets of ketchup from afar. During religious festivals or the auspicious Hindu months for weddings, these sachets practically fly off the wires.

This isn't a poor thing—this is an aspirational market thing. On a per-drop basis, this shampoo is outrageously priced, but in such small volumes, it's affordable as a splurge. This micro-aspirational culture was illustrated by an Airtel commercial running constantly in late 2009 that showed a well-dressed, pretty Indian woman walking by a fancy bakery and admiring an elaborate cake. She walks in and the grumpy baker takes the cake out of the counter and shows her the price tag. She mimes that she would like a tiny slice. He frowns. She makes a pleading face. And in the next scene she's walking out beaming and eating a microscopic slice of cake.

This amuse-bouche market is the most sure-fire way that companies have found to make huge money on India's 1.1 billion-person but unequal market. It's the perfect bite-sized chunk for a country where an urban crush and a flood of multinational jobs have conspired to make everyone want the city, Zippo-flipping lifestyle, even if only a small percentage can afford it. The woman in the Airtel ad isn't depicted as poor or cheap; she simply *wants* a tiny slice.

Smart entrepreneurs in India are taking this microconcept and pushing it further. Increasingly things aren't marketed in a physical packet, they're marketed virtually over the most mundane, prepaid cell phone. After all, telecommunications is one of the only parts of India's modern infrastructure that works, and part of that is because it exploits this microeconomy with network plans that sell airtime by the *paisa*, which is worth less than the value of one penny.

While much of the Western world obsesses with glitzy time-wasting games sold over $300 smart phones, a growing crop of Indian entrepreneurs can do things with the most basic Nokia that would blow your mind. SMS, numerical dialing, and in some cases call centers and voice recognition software are for India what the dial-up Internet was in the West in the late 1990s—only it's more powerful because up until now nothing has connected the country.

A large education and technology company called IL&FS has an experimental product that teaches English lessons over the phone. You listen, speak English back, and dial numbers to answer multiple-choice questions. Whole groups of teenaged girls gather in villages on hot summer nights, put a cell phone on speaker, and learn English together, visions of high-paid jobs dancing in their heads.

A company called redBus.in aggregates and sells bus tickets. It's a huge market in India, with some 750,000 tickets sold daily through 3,000 different agents. The company only took off once the founders accepted that they weren't a Web company; rather, they were a company that sold bus tickets over any medium. More than half of the thousands of tickets redBus sells every day are sold over cell phones. It's such an important delivery channel that redBus' co-founder and CEO Phanindra Sama insists on building regional call centers throughout the country to make sure the operators know the local routes, language, and slang. (In a nod to the earlier chapter's point about how well India uses connections, redBus got this advice through a mentor in the TiE network and was funded by Pravin Gandhi's venture fund.)

A company called SMS GupShup is building something that's a cross between a social network, Twitter, and the Yahoo! Groups application, all for basic mobile phones. The founder, Beerud Sheth, was ranked first when he took the IIT exam and got his pick of schools and majors. He went to IIT Mumbai, and the next logical step was MIT in the United States for grad school. He went to Wall Street instead, and in the late 1990s, he cofounded an online talent marketplace called eLance and moved to Silicon Valley, his team wearing orange eLance shirts and popping champagne bottles on the flight.

Sheth has put those Valley connections to good use. SMS GupShup has raised an impressive $37 million in Silicon Valley venture capital and has 32 million users. But that's nothing compared to the opportunity. While the Web has 1.5 billion users worldwide, mobile has more than double that. In the emerging world, even those who have Web access only get it an hour or two per day, versus 24-hour access with a phone and a far better connection. But most mobile versions of Web sites don't work on basic phones, making users hungry for more interactive functionality. The more functionality they get over their mobile, the less incentive they have to switch to computers, Sheth says.

The money is there, too—the same way it is for Pantene, in micro-aspirational chunks. The good and bad of text messages is that they cost money. That means a company like SMS GupShup—which is sending hundreds of millions of messages per month—is expensive to build out, but people are used to being charged to send a message, as opposed to the Web, where the expectation is that everything is free. Low-tech, pooh-poohed SMS generates about $100 billion in annual revenues, where the consumer Web generates just $75 billion, and $25 billion of that goes to Google, Sheth argues.

The ambitious Sheth looks at this situation and sees the opportunity to build the Yahoo! of mobile. Even with its slumping stock price, Yahoo! is still one of the largest media properties ever created, with half a billion unique users coming to its homepage every month. "We could be the world's largest social phenomenon in a way you can't on the Web," Sheth says. "When societies adopt media that becomes the standard, it's hard to switch. There's a Valley-centric view that mobile is a second-class experience, but SMS is the social glue of the emerging world."

Several miles south of Sheth's offices in Mumbai, a company called Justdial is the Google equivalent for the mobile phone nation. People think of something they are looking for—a phone number, a restaurant, a category like "doctor"—and call Justdial as automatically as someone online would enter a word in Google. It promises an answer within 30 seconds, and you can be connected, texted, or e-mailed the information for free. The company generates

more than $30 million in annual revenues for the audio equiva-
lent of Google's paid search ads. That is small on a global scale, but
Justdial's reach is huge in India, answering close to 100 million calls
per year, growing at a rate of 40 percent annually. Said one woman
who has never used a computer: "Before I can think of what I'm
looking for, I'm calling them."

The company was started by an entrepreneur named VSS Mani,
who dropped out of school, which is downright shocking in
education-centric India. He first tried to start this company in the
late 1980s, at least a decade too early and well before India's telecom
explosion. Years later, when he tried again, he had to apply for a
landline and wait several years before he could open the business.
After years of fits and starts, he could only afford a 300-square-foot
office in downtown Mumbai. "I didn't care as long as I had the
address on my business card," he says. When the late 1990s hit,
everyone argued that the Internet was the new thing, not phone calls,
and Mani changed his business under pressure. But the Internet
didn't take off broadly in India, and mobile adoption soared. He'd
been right all along and pulled the business back to its roots.

Mani insists there's no substitute for a human being answering the phone, armed with powerful software. In 2010, Justdial
has pulled what might be an India digital first, expanding into the
United States. In March, the company launched 1-800-JUSTDIAL,
a direct volley against 411 services, which increasingly use voice
recognition software to connect people to businesses. The plan
is to launch local call centers in poor areas of the United States.
Ironically, an Indian company will be bringing call center jobs to
the United States. It may be ambitious, but Mani has raised $46
million from Tiger Ventures, SAIF, and Silicon Valley powerhouse
Sequoia Capital, which funded Google early on. The entire sum is
still in the bank. Justdial has reached this point off of its own revenues and Mani's original, paltry $1,000 investment.

With such an emphasis on voice calls, it's a good thing call centers
are a core Indian competency. Like BYD and CK Telecom in China,

these companies aren't outsourcing the tasks their country has excelled at providing; they are using them as endemic advantages. A growing number of Indians are getting call center jobs from Indian companies, not American ones. And, like BYD and CK Telecom, companies like redBus, SMS GupShup, and Justdial are actually building products and services for themselves, not for the West.

Back in Lal's store, he pulls out a stack of little green booklets and slaps them on the counter in front of Abhishek Sinha, exclaiming something in Hindi. Sinha is starting a company called Eko India Financial Services, and this stack of books full of crossed-out codes is good news. It means Eko's mobile phone bank accounts—Lal's newest product in his micro-arsenal—are selling fast.

Eko's bank accounts don't try to be everything to everyone. It aims squarely at the unbanked—some 60 percent of India's huge population. There are no extra bells and whistles with Eko's service because there's no room for them, and at the end of the day, probably little need for them. The accounts are actually held by the State Bank of India, which insures up to 100,000 rupees per account, but Eko's customers don't ever go into banks. The tellers are grocers like Lal—the benign feudal warlords of every street and village in India. Eko just seeks to give this already trusted, daily-visited vendor one more thing to sell.

The interface is simple enough for anyone to use, regardless of language or literacy. Just like filling out a check requires you to enter the payee, how much you are paying, and sign it, Eko's transactions have the same three elements. Eko customers type the bank's short code, then an asterisk, then the mobile number of the person being paid, then an asterisk, then the amount, then another asterisk. Then comes the signature. That's the tricky part, but also the most important, because the account is solely on phones, which can be stolen.

Sinha wanted to come up with a cost-effective equivalent of a digital RSA token, so he created a paper version of it. Account holders get little booklets with pages of 11-digit codes. Seven digits of the code are random numbers, with four randomly placed black marks. The customer enters a PIN code wherever the black marks are, and each code can be used once. So even if the booklet is stolen, the account can't be accessed. There's a VeriSign logo on each booklet. Sinha reached out to the security experts to see if they could come up with a better solution, but instead they just endorsed his approach.

There are a lot of ingenious things about this seemingly simple business. For one thing, nearly everyone in India's cities has a cell phone even if they don't have a home, income, power, or access to clean water. So if you want banking to be broad based, it's the only possible medium. And with literacy rates of 73 percent for men and 48 percent for women, even an SMS system would be a challenge, but everyone can dial numbers.

Making vendors like Lal the tellers of Eko's virtual bank is crucial to wide adoption. These vendors are the hub of India's poorer economies, typically extending credit when even a sachet of shampoo is too expensive, essentially acting like trusted bankers already. Lal has only been opening up Eko bank accounts for about five months, and business is growing. He slides Sinha a handwritten ledger showing the day's volume—28,000 rupees deposited and 30,000 rupees withdrawn. Lal gets a tiny cut of each transaction, ensuring he'll keep pushing the accounts. He is looking at Sinha with a self-satisfied, smug grin. And why not? Even for the surging microeconomy, Lal is a "rock star," says Sinha.

Eko has not been an easy company to build. There's a cost-time trade-off. For two years, Eko was partnering with a third party who sells multiple things through the corner grocer already. But evangelizing the product takes more handholding, so accounts weren't growing fast enough. Since November 2009, Eko has taken over the management of these grocer accounts, assigning employees to each neighborhood and investing in street promotions, bedecking stores with signage and blaring its Bollywood-esque jingle that extols the virtues of banking. Eko had just 6,000 accounts before the switch in strategy. It added 10,000 in January 2010 and was soon adding 20,000 accounts per month.

But costs are going up, too. Sinha, who made some money founding a previous company, Six DEE Telecom Solutions, bootstrapped Eko, along with a $1.78 million grant from the World Bank and The Gates Foundation. But in 2010 that money was running low, and finding more wasn't easy. VCs in India like to back proven companies, and Eko takes more money to prove it can be big.

Sinha talks about the days after he sold his last company. He made more money in his early thirties than most of his family ever had. But a funny thing happened as he repaid his loans, gave raises to his domestic staff, and took his wife on the honeymoon they never had: his aspiration level went up. He broke that Indian curse of contentment. Suddenly, he wanted more. Sinha says, "I realized my duty is to disrupt other people's aspiration levels." "Why shouldn't we all have big dreams? People are afraid to dream, but that's going to change and Eko is going to play a role in that. No more putting money in a jar, no more sewing money into a false pocket inside of their shirts, no more money under the mattress. The unbanked poor in India will only have real control over their financial future when the cash is out of everyone's physical reach."

Money aside, Sinha felt like a failure when he sold his last company. He was trying to build something big, not just make money. The company had several near-death experiences, and each time he resurrected it. Finally, in 2005, someone wanted to buy the business, and his investors wanted to sell. He fought it at first but eventually gave in. "It took me six months to get over it," he says. "I left with a lot of pain in my heart."

Now, with Eko, he's not worried about raising more money because he's been more desperate than this before. "I'm not proud to say I've defaulted on every credit card and on every loan I've ever had," he says. "I've paid bribes to get more credit. After a point in time you stop worrying. You get to know you're a lucky guy and push yourself further."

Ironically, by getting intensely local, India is digitally stretching across its unconnected, mostly impoverished, half-illiterate nation the way the British did in colonial times with the railroad, and the impact on people's lives is no less vivid. As the country signs up millions more mobile users per month, the trend is reaching deeper into the villages.

Finding a way to modernize the villages is key to making life better in India. Unlike China, Indian cities don't have the infrastructure to support a full-scale migration, nor does India have a powerful, autocratic government that can mold new satellite cities out of nothing. Delhi tried with Gurgaon, a city constructed so haphazardly that most of the companies operating there run off generators. India isn't 10 years behind China, as many pundits say. What worked for China won't work in India. India has to find another path to modernity. Even Mahatma Gandhi used to say: If you want to change India, change the villages.

Too high-minded social thinking for greed-based entrepreneurs? Hardly. The villages are where the mass market is in India. And if the country can crack the sachet equivalent of the digital revolution, it will have a leg up on bridging the same divide in Africa, Southeast Asia, and any corner of the world where the Web is experienced over a pay-as-you-go monthly phone.

∽

"You've arrived in the village," Ravi Ghate said as our SUV pulled into Hiware Bazar's community center parking lot, somewhere in the middle of the Maharashtra plateau.

"Yeah, I know," I said, looking around. I mean, I didn't really know what Hiware Bazar would look like, but I assumed that since the car stopped rattling down dirt roads and weaving in and out of carts, cows, and mopeds in the random markets that would sprout up every 50 kilometers, we were at the next village. The fact that my grip had finally loosened on the car's "oh-shit bar" had been my cue most of the day.

"No, look," he said and showed me his cell phone. There was a 140-character news story that had just been pushed to Hiware Bazar's 1,350 residents' phones telling them in Marathi that U.S. reporter Sarah Lacy had arrived in the village.

I was hardly the first. This village has been featured in dozens of news articles, on the BBC and the Discovery Channel. It used to be crippled by drought, erosion, poverty, and devastation. Then, 20 years ago, it restructured its town council and started to take control of its future. Through dozens of different techniques—like terracing of land and storing rainwater during the monsoons— Hiware Bazar went from wasteland to arable land. You can literally see the village's border, where the grass goes from brown to green.

The village didn't stop there: It voted that every house had to use a toilet and banned cows from grazing freely, curtailing contamination of ground water. Likewise, there's no trash on the streets. It's one of the only places in India where you can breathe in deeply and smell nothing but clean air. With almost none of the sanitation issues that plague Indian cities and villages alike, Hiware Bazar will give any visitor 100 rupees if they find a single mosquito. And if a visitor has to pump a well more than once to get a clear stream of water, they also get 100 rupees.

The village built better schools, has regular health drives to test for heart and blood pressure problems, put the property in the women's names because they live longer, and built a mosque for the one Muslim family who lives there. Once a month, the town gathers in the square and votes on everything. Because everyone gets a vote, everyone upholds the rules.

Twenty years ago, people had to leave Hiware Bazar to make a living. Now everyone wants to get in, and the town has passed rules saying that only those living there now or born there can be residents. Back in 1995, only 12 families were above the poverty line. Now, only three are below it. Farmers growing onions, potatoes, peas, and tomatoes are even using the Hiware Bazar brand at the market to fetch a higher price. And they've discovered new crops.

Our guide plucked some woodsy looking bark and held it up to my nose. I breathed in an unexpected flowery, earthy smell. "Used for perfume in the U.S.," he said. In a stunning reversal, the village is home to more than 50 rupee millionaires today.

The one thing this town lacks is the Internet. "The tower is there," my guide says in Maranthi, pointing to a tower in the distance. "It's just not working." So until a few years ago, town announcements were made over a series of loud speakers. Today the residents are connected by text message. The company that's done this is called SMSOne, and its founded by Ravi Ghate, an uneducated idealist who once sold berries and flags by the side of the road. "Those kids you tell to 'Go away,'" he says, shooing an imaginary boy. "That is the boy I was."

SMSOne is basically a very local newsletter delivered over SMS. Hiwar Bazaar is a tight community that wasn't immediately convinced it needed SMSOne. Then one day, the Indian equivalent of the DMV came to the village to give out driver's licenses. "The regional transport authority is ten times worse than your DMV," Ghate says, and from what I know of Indian bureaucracy, I wonder if he's *understating* it. Normally it would take days of lost work to travel to the office and get a license. But on this day, the office was coming to them. People who had SMSOne knew about it in advance, and in one day, the regional transport authority gave out 150 licenses. Those who didn't have SMSOne either heard about it late and frantically ran in from farms to get a license or missed out completely. After that, most of the town was sold on the service. Today in Hiware Bazar even wedding invitations go out over SMSOne.

Most of SMSOne's villages look more like the Hiware Bazar before picture of 20 years ago. They lack Internet, but also TV, local papers, and frequently electricity. A phone is all they have, and SMSOne is their only way to get highly relevant, sometimes lifesaving information. It can give farmers instant updates about crop pricing or news of a seed delivery a town away. In many places, government water pipes are only turned on once a week and inconsistently at that. Residents have to wait and then rush every basin, tub, and kerosene can they own to the pipe to stock up. If they miss it, they get no water that week. Now in SMSOne villages, they get a text message telling them when the water is going to be turned on.

The amazing part is that this is a for-profit startup. Ghate goes to a village and scouts out an unemployed teen or 20-something, preferably one who has experience as a street vendor or shilling for local politicians. The kid pays Ghate 1,000 rupees (or about $20) for the franchise rights to be the local reporter for that village. He goes door to door signing up 1,000 names and phone numbers and then mails these paper slips to Ghate. Ghate enters it all in his databases and those new "subscribers" get a text introducing the kid as their village's reporter. The reporter texts his stories in to Ghate, and Ghate pushes them out to subscribers. SMSOne started out free but now charges users 12 rupees per year for the service to help defray the messaging costs.

The bulk of the revenues come from advertising, like any other media property. The local editors sell short 40-character ads to local shops like Lal's, mom-and-pop service providers in the village, and local politicians running for office. On the traditional Web, Google used paid search ads to tap into a huge market by giving small businesses a measurable, affordable way to reach potential customers. SMSOne is trying to do something similar. Just like Pantene and the corner grocer found a way to sell shampoo in the slums, Ghate has found a way to sell advertising to thousands of businesses that never advertised before because there was no appropriate micro-medium.

The biggest cost is finding those reporters. In some villages, Ghate's crew spent thousands of rupees scouting, training, and replacing local reporters, who only paid them a 1,000 rupee franchise fee. That's not sustainable in a business charging for microads, and Ghate is not running a nonprofit. That lead to a new idea: SMSOne in schools.

Ghate is rolling out an education version of the newsletters, which makes school announcements like lectures, tests, and regional contests, to the hundreds of colleges and universities in the

Pune district. "One college has 1,000 students that belong to fifty villages," Ghate says excitedly. The school nominates 20 students to be the reporters, and upon graduation, Ghate picks one or two and offers them a job as the reporter in their home villages.

His plan is to leverage this hiring channel to build a knowledge grid in the next three years throughout India at a college, village, and district level—all connected by SMS. Beyond news and micro-ads, SMSOne could eventually get into classifieds. It could be a human-powered Craigslist or eBay, where someone in a Village needs something, pays the reporter to send a message out, and the reporter finds it. "Connect the boy, connect the family, connect the village, connect the boy, connect the family, connect the village," Ghate says, as if it's a mantra. If he does this, he connects India, too.

For a micro-business, SMSOne is a huge vision. Roughly two-thirds of India's 1.1 billion people live in villages. Half of them lack all-weather roads, and many lack access to basic health care and education.[1] Bringing India's 680,000 villages into the modern age seems impossible for a government that can't even build sewer systems in India's largest cities. It'll be up to entrepreneurs like Ghate to make life better for the bulk of unconnected Indians.

And unlike nearly every other Indian entrepreneur I've met, Ghate does not want money from venture capitalists. He tried meeting with them. After I wrote about him on TechCrunch in 2009, he got flooded with press and investor calls. "They eat at my head!" he says, doing a motion of swatting away invisible birds swarming him. "All those Silicon Valley ideas, they are not applicable here." Specifically, he didn't like the idea that a startup needed an experienced management team—i.e., not Ghate and the motley crew he assembled from chance meetings in villages and bus stations.

Ghate can come across as awkward in a boardroom. He formally prefaces every sentence with "Ma'am" but informally always writes "you" as "u" and "please" as "plz" even when he's not texting. He even writes that way on press releases on his Web site. He shrugs, saying, "Our site is written for the people, not the venture capitalists."

But in a village Ghate is in his element: parts politician, celebrity, activist, and shrewd CEO. He knows the residents' and students' personal stories by heart, teases them, and charms them. When he talks to a town council, he has them in the palm of his hand. We visited half a dozen villages together and, like a fish story, my credentials got more exaggerated each time. "I am telling them you are the most famous reporter in the world," he'd whisper to me in English, winking. Villagers would silently lift up their Nokias and snap photos of me. When we were running late for a meeting and our next appointment demanded to know how much longer it would be, Ghate gave the intentionally vague answer, "Go get a lime juice and talk to the guys, and by the time you're done we'll be there."

But most importantly, he knows how to get things done in this relationship-driven, inefficient world. "What trouble they give us I can't explain," he says about signing up colleges over the past few months. "We have to visit any college three times to get anything done, and they *enjoy* putting us through this. What I am bearing I cannot tell." Today, he's in a nice car with a driver, but only because I'm with him. Normally he's taking the bus and staying in $5-per-night hotel rooms. "These are my people," he says.

But once a community signs up for SMSOne, the loyalty makes that hassle worth it. It has an impact beyond each micro-story, and in the tumult of India's cruel hand-to-mouth existence, it has united people. I spent an evening following an SMSOne reporter named Anil through a slum on the outskirts of Pune. We wound our way from the tire shop where elderly men gather to sound off about issues of the day, to the temples, to the dirty patch by the river where women lay out vegetables on blankets to make their living, to the circuitous back streets where people live in one-room hovels on less than $2 per day.

This is a migrant neighborhood trapped in the modern Indian struggle for life, and, before SMSOne, the residents all told me they didn't know or care much about one another. As the local editor, Anil had his work cut out for him. He wound up writing his first story before he'd even finished collecting the local numbers, when he discovered that one of those unnamed women selling vegetables by the side of the road had tried to poison herself. She felt trapped by her economic situation, hopeless that things would never get any easier. Anil found her, rushed her near-lifeless body to the hospital, and then manually typed in each subscriber's phone number to send a story asking for help. The community rallied around her, chipping in rupees to pay her medical bills, convincing her that her life mattered. Standing in her doorway of cracking, pale blue paint with babies crying in the background, she told me that life still isn't easy, but things are better now.

This community has dozens of stories like this: the woman who had blood cancer and needed donors, the little girl born with a hole in her heart whose parents couldn't afford surgery, and the community that continually pitches in to help people once they read about them in these 140-character bursts. The men in the tire shop told me that SMSOne had changed the makeup of the sprawling neighborhood. The other day, someone was looting a store, and several men rushed over to stop them, where before they likely would have kept walking. Anil wrote their story and called them heroes. Walking through this slum for hours, hearing dramatic stories like these over and over again, it was striking how similar they all started to sound. A lot of Western pundits argue that technology isn't what India needs when basics like jobs and water are in such short supply. That's why rich people shouldn't be the ones making the decisions about what poor people need. Just as a hot meal, clean water, or a U.S. dollar can take on a meaning the rich can't understand in a poor neighborhood, so too can basic technologies that connect people to one another.

Ghate's frustrations with VCs have made him only more determined, not just to prove this can be done but to prove *he* can do it. "I am a piece of carbon and all of these challenges and hate words are polishing me up to become a diamond," he says. You could argue that Ghate is the type of entrepreneur that takes India into the future, not the guys writing code for a multinational and dreaming of sports cars. He has that old-world Jugaad, but he is finding new ways to make it scale. He is content in his personal life like a good Hindu, but he wants more in business. Ghate sums up this odd mix of old-world Hinduism and ambitious 21st-century capitalism when he says, "I always ask God for ultimate things. God is a billionaire; why ask for millions?"

∞

Companies like Justdial, redBus, SMS GupShup, Eko India Financial Services, and SMSOne grow in two obvious ways. The first is by more people with cell phones using their services. The second, longer-term strategy is for this cell phone infrastructure to reach even more Indians.

The work of Airtel and Reliance aside, there are still Indians that mobile carriers can't reach. Not everyone can pay $6 per month. Not content with what the country's entrepreneurs have pulled off so far, Rajiv Mehrotra thinks cell phones should be profitable on average revenues of less than $2 per user. And he's got a plan. It's not to squeeze more costs out of the business model the way the big companies have already tried, because there's no more to squeeze. Instead, Mehrotra is starting fresh.

Mehrotra's company, VNL, has tackled all three of the problems with deep rural mobile access. Connectivity: By stripping out unnecessary things like 3G access, VNL can extend the basic mobile voice and data signal 100 kilometers with a simple antenna. Power: The base stations are totally solar powered, so no electricity is no problem. Maintenance and installation: VNL's base stations are Ikea-like easy to assemble. They come with pictorial instructions and a wrench and take anyone just a few hours to put together. One man I met was out when his base station arrived, and his nosy neighbors set it up for him by the time he got back home.

These three factors are interrelated: a simpler device, for instance, can run on just one solar panel, and all three factors help with cost. Now, mobile operators can actually turn a profit on a place they never thought they'd reach.

Typically, the base stations are installed on a villager's roof for a fee. In the case of the aforementioned man, he's gotten more respect among his peers and is frequently the one called—literally now—to settle disputes. The impact on the 500 people in his small village is profound. Everyone carries his or her phones everywhere. A baby toddling around in the dirt even had a pink, plastic, candy-filled mobile phone around his neck.

Some of the results are obvious or mundane. Almost everyone says the first call they made was to far-flung family. Wives will call husbands who are out in the fields when it's time to come in and eat, rather than trudging out to get them, allowing them to focus on kids and the housework. Just like in the United States, kids grab their parents' phones as soon as they come into the house and look for games they can play.

Other times the result is more profound. One woman I spoke with was a widow with six kids and 21 grandchildren. (So many, she actually had to ask someone else how many she had.) As grand-kids clambered in and out of her lap and she took a long pull off a rusty hookah, she explained that she gets pension checks from the government, but the delivery used to be spotty. Before she got a phone, she had no recourse but to walk six kilometers to the near-est payphone and hope they answered, because there was no way to call her back. Twice she had to travel to Delhi to inquire about it. Not exactly something she enjoyed, having lived her whole life in this village. Now she can call the office and give them an earful. Not surprisingly, the checks have started to come more regularly.

Another man, one village over, told me he felt more connected to the rest of India as a result of having his phone. His village is surrounded by mountains, and he said that he'd felt "imprisoned" and cut off, despite being just a few hours' drive from Delhi. Now he has a renewed interest in politics and what's happening in other villages and the country at large. This man had only had his phone for six months, but he said, "since the day I got this, my life has already changed."

Mehrotra says it's already having a ripple effect on the politics of Rajasthan—the state between Pakistan and India where VNL did its first installations. Politicians come through and make promises, and now villagers demand their cell phone numbers and call to check up on whether those promises are kept. "They have to be accountable," Mehrotra says. "They can't wriggle out."

These phones are not just a nice-to-have accessory anymore; they've quickly become a must-have for these villages, and the phones are deeply tied to the way people make money, participate in their government, and retain close family relationships. And these ripple effects are only beginning. Think of what the impact will be when there are better programs for marketing crops, saving money, and even learning and game playing rolled out on these very basic phones. Mehrotra says there are government subsidies for generators that run on cow dung now that few villagers know about. Phones could change that. "What is the one thing you saw in excess in the villages?" Mehrotra says. "Cow dung!" He's not kidding. It's dried in patties and stored in little huts also made of cow dung that are etched with decorative flower designs. Cow dung is burned as a vital source of fuel in places where wood and coal is a luxury.

Life will always be different in a village than in a city, but India can at least gain some basic common denominators between the two. And the more people with phones, the more people who can use services like Justdial to find information, buy tickets from Redbus to travel to see relatives, learn English using IL&FS, get news via SMSOne, or get bank accounts with Eko. Suddenly, life opens up. It's a literal dial-up Internet in a place that has nothing.

No one believed Mehrotra could pull this off, but he's one of those rare combinations in an entrepreneur who knows the technology, product side of things and wheeling-dealing, business side of things. And like Ghate, Mehrotra knows villages. He'd already built businesses rolling out satellite TV and landlines to rural areas. But Mehrotra thinks this company will have a bigger impact than anything else he's done before, and it is the one with the real potential to go global.

Villages in Africa are an obvious fit, but there are even vast reaches of the United States that have no mobile access. VNL is already getting calls from ski resorts and ranches that are interested in getting their own base stations for the comfort of high-end visitors. "It's $150,000 for the whole thing and it covers thousands of acres," Mehrotra says. He doesn't see it working in European countries, China, Japan, and Korea, but any other country in the world is in his sights. "World population is 6.5 billion people, and only 3 billion have phones," he says.

Mehrotra is every bit the mogul in fancy suits and baby blue ties, holed up in a fortress of an office, and driven around in expensive cars. His sprawling estate houses generations of his family, and his children too are all building companies. He has built his fortune from nothing, starting out when he was 10 years old assembling and selling transistor radios by the side of the road.

Nothing rattles him. We did an interview lurching through Delhi rush hour traffic, while I was in the grips of Delhi belly. I told him I thought I was going to be sick, and he coolly pulled a mailing envelope out of his seat-back pocket, removed the document inside, and handed it to me. As I vomited—repeatedly—into the envelope, he reached into a secret refrigerated panel and offered me a Diet Coke as he kept talking. Similarly, he bats away questions about business model, money, and competition like India's ever-present mini-swarm of mosquitoes and gnats.

"Business model is easy, you just build something people want."

"Money is the easiest thing in the world to make."

"Competition is nothing. The day you get a brother or sister, your competition is born."

Because no one believed Mehrotra could do this, he had to fund it himself, and it was not cheap. The self-made billionaire has invested more than $100 million in the last five years and is still investing more. He says it was the only way. Once he built it, he'd take equipment and operator executives out to see it, and they still couldn't believe it. They were making calls from different areas of the village trying to find pockets without a signal. "They were climbing on the antenna and shaking it like monkeys trying to break it and they couldn't," Mehrotra says.

The operators love VNL because it cheaply expands their existing footprint. The equipment makers aren't so sure. In theory, VNL isn't competing with them because it isn't selling equipment to the cities. Now that VNL has proved this model works, could a larger established vendor steal the market? The best chance of that would likely come from a Chinese powerhouse like Huawei. That said, any vendor that builds such a low-cost solution will risk eroding its higher-priced systems designed for urban areas. "They'll say 'Give it to me in the city, too.' We are the bottom of the bottom," boasts Mehrotra, practically daring competitors to try to play his low-cost, solar-powered, super-durability game.

Once everyone saw it could work, VNL became a global, save-the-earth, save-the-poor darling. The World Economic Forum named it one of 26 Technology Pioneers, and in 2010, VNL won the Mobile World Congress's Green Mobile Award. *Time* called it a "Tech Pioneer That Will Change Your Life," and *Fast Company* named it one of the 50 Most Innovative Companies in the world.

Mehrotra hopes the phones will do something beyond fulfilling basic needs. He hopes they'll enable villagers to become entrepreneurs themselves, whether that means using phones to get better prices on crops or something bigger. Mehrotra has a familiar gripe about Indians: "A level of satisfaction comes fast, and we don't make it big." Mehrotra gets exhausted talking about this issue of not making anything. "We don't have any product companies," he says, on a rant now. "Show me one. And don't show me a foreign company that's had a product designed here. None of us own our intellectual property."

He tells the familiar story of three baskets of crabs at a market: one from China, one from Korea, and one from India. The first two have lids on them, but the Indian basket is open. Why?

Because if one Indian crab tries to crawl out, the others pull it back down. It's curious that I hear this analogy so much in India, when I know so many successful Valley-based Indians who work to lift other Indians immigrants up, in ways other minorities—even women entrepreneurs—have not. Like the big, sprawling family analogy, somehow Indians can band together when they're against the world, but they pull at each other when they're on their own turf.

Mehrotra is hoping technology can show the crabs the way out, that the people who have been left out of the services boom will focus on their own futures and stop pulling each other down. That's the bigger bet he's making with his $100 million investment in VNL, and it's a lot of pressure to put on a mobile phone network. But democracy only works when people have a voice, and the phone is the only thing in India that gives a voice to a big swath of the population. The strength of India's democracy isn't found in the lackluster, frequently corrupt politicians and bureaucrats. It's found in the Indians who are never shy about voicing an opinion and demand fair representation.

India won't become a superpower until the whole country can prosper, not just the small percentage who work in multinational call centers and consulting firms. Gandhi was right, in a weird modern way. It is all about the villages. Because India has no authoritarian government to lift everyone up, the country has to lift itself up through entrepreneurship.

Dysfunctional, messy India could have the emerging world's last laugh. Not only does it have a huge domestic market, but if you can modernize India, you can modernize anyplace. That means India's entrepreneurs could understand the business challenges and solutions in even less developed markets in Africa and Southeast Asia in a way developed countries like the United States and autocratic countries like China never will. India's future could be less about doing the work the West doesn't want and more about solving problems that newer democracies are just now facing.

Brazil

8

Do You Know Who You Are Talking To?

*I*t's surprising how frequently colonialismcomes up when you're talking about modern entrepreneurship. Consider Brazil and the United States: Both are huge landmasses with abundant natural resources and large populations. Both were originally inhabited by tribes of Native Americans. Both were explored, conquered, and colonized by Europeans, and both got independence around the same time. Both brought slaves from Africa, and both freed them around the same time, too.

Both are isolationist, and both think they are the most important country on earth, or at least on their respective continents. Each can talk smack about itself, but neither let anyone else. There's a cultural cliché that when affronted, an entitled Brazilian will say "Do you know who you are talking to?" By contrast, the cliché of an affronted entitled American is "Who do you think you are?"[1] One implies a society where status buys favors, the other implies a society where everyone feels entitled to favors, but it's a subtle difference. It's as if America is Brazil's bizarro world and Brazil is America's.

With so much shared history and swagger, how is it that America is a modern-yet-aging superpower and Brazil is still an emerging market? The common answer Brazilians give has to do with the differences between being colonized by the English and the Portuguese. The United States inherited the hard-driving Protestant work ethic, compared to the more contented, veil-of-tears worldview of a Portuguese Catholic.

But it's not just who colonized you that matters. After all, the English colonized India too, and the United States has far more in common with Brazil. The bigger difference is *the way* the English colonized America. It wasn't just to plunder natural resources; the settlers sought to create a new country. The English brought their families with them to America. The birth of Virginia Dare—the first English baby born in the new world—is written about in history books as a seminal moment for the settlers. Meanwhile, Brazil was a place the Portuguese went to do a job. Nearly half of all African slaves transported to the Americas went to Brazil, far more than any other country.[2]

While some typically English values were instilled in the United States early on, many attitudes were explicitly a reaction against the way things were done in the United Kingdom. In corporate terms, it's the difference between an executive buying a disruptive startup and quitting his job to start one.

Post-colonization, the biggest reason Brazil—and Latin America as a whole—developed differently was largely political, thanks to a wave of dictators, coups, runaway inflation, and general instability. For the latter part of the 20th century, Brazil wasn't nearly as backward as India or China in terms of infrastructure, especially in its major cities, but it was nowhere near as advanced as the United States. If China and India were huge sleeping giants, Brazil was more of a groggy giant. That means it doesn't have the same greenfield opportunities of those Asian countries today, but there is also less work to be done to give people basic economic dignity.

Where the infrastructure breaks down, it's more that it's decaying—like in parts of the United States—rather than being nonexistent, as it is in India today and in China 10 years ago. "Brazil, unlike Russia, India, and China, with which it is constantly compared as a member of the BRIC group of big emerging nations, is not only a mature, stable and diversified economy but also one largely unthreatened by social, demographic or economic upheavals,"[3] wrote the *Financial Times* in 2009.

Much of the Western world forgot about South America for the last few decades, with the socially conscious press focusing more on Africa and the business press focusing more on Asia. But suddenly, in 2009, Brazil became scorching hot. Economically, the country was basking in a huge discovery of oil, and many of its other commodity markets were taking off, too. Brazil already made up some 60 percent of South America's economy and by most measures surpassed Canada as the second largest economy in the Americas.[4] The $8 billion IPO of the Brazilian arm of Santander Bank was one of the biggest global financial events in a bleak year of worldwide recession.

Politically, the world was encouraged by President Luiz Inácio Lula da Silva's peaceful transference of power from his rightist predecessor Fernando Henrique Cardoso—and the fact that Lula didn't change much policy-wise. Lula was an uneducated former union leader, and his victory was so feared by foreign investors that Brazil's credit rating plunged as soon as he took office, but much-talked-about policy moves like more restrictive labor laws were never implemented. Lula quickly realized that for Brazil to succeed, it needed to appease the international capitalist world—a major milestone for the go-it-alone nation.

The government has also made impressive strides when it comes to Brazil's economic inequality. The percentage of the population that makes less than $2 per day fell from 22 percent to just 9 percent from 2003 to 2008. And those still under the poverty line are making 22 percent more than they were back in 2002, according to the World Bank.

When Rio de Janeiro won the right to host the 2014 World Cup and beat out Chicago, Tokyo, and Madrid to host the 2016 Olympics, Brazil's confidence and world image swelled. Entering a new decade, it was clear to the world that something big was happening in Brazil. But what exactly?

Brazil's economic opportunity is difficult to quantify. Hype aside, it has grown far slower than its BRIC counterparts. Brazil has invested heavily in social, political, and economic stability, which has come at the price of sheer economic growth. Brazil isn't saving or investing enough of its income, and productivity is lagging, Goldman Sachs griped in 2005. Others complain that Brazil is still too closed in its trade relations, and its labor and tax laws are still too antibusiness. That said, there are growing opportunities when it comes to building consumer products for Brazil's new middle class and a huge potential to use technology to reinvent its agricultural and energy sector.

The question is whether local entrepreneurs will rise to those challenges. Unlike in Israel, China, and India, there's scant early-stage venture capital flowing into Brazil, and rival Argentina is home to the only Latin American company to go public on the NASDAQ—mercadoLibre, an eBay-like ecommerce marketplace. For a long time there wasn't even a Portuguese word for "entrepreneur." Money was something you had or you didn't in Brazilian culture, and people who made their fortunes quickly were eyed suspiciously. In telenovelas, the entrepreneur is always the villain.

Brazil isn't a rapidly rising economic tide lifting all boats like China. It's not even a slowly rising economic tide that will one day lift boats like India. Nor is it a place that overperforms economically thanks to smart policy and a willingness to take risk like Israel. That's led to an entrepreneurship wave that's a hodgepodge of up-and-coming companies that seemingly have little in common with one another. And unlike Israel, China, and India, the United States is largely being left out of their rise.

But Brazil has one very big thing going for it that I didn't find in any other country: The poor in Brazil dream big.

⌒∞⌒

"Oh! Those are my friends," Marco Gomes says, making a sharp U-turn. We're in the beat-up white Fiat he drove when he lived in Gama, and a decal reading "Jesus: The Secret to Peace" in Portuguese is still on the dash. Gomes doubles back to a park where four gangly, shirtless boys are jumping off of different structures. It's almost dusk on a Saturday night, and as we swing past some nearby teens, Gomes notes the cruising is already underway. "Gama's dating scene," he says, nodding in their direction. "The men stop, turn their music up, the girls dance, and they pick one."

His friends were doing *parkour*, an urban gymnastics sport popularized online. Gomes walks up, and they all smile.

"Hey, little faggot," one says in Portuguese, giving him a sideways slapping high-five that turns into a hug.

"Go fuck yourself," Gomes replies. It's shocking language for a devout Christian, but this isn't the Brazil you see on postcards. When Gomes was growing up here, certain blocks were off limits, marked by groups of men sweating in the blistering sun, guns strapped to their shoulders. Sometimes those men were drug dealers, and sometimes they were cops. Gomes didn't like to get close enough to find out. Sounding tough is the first step toward not getting shot. Although, Gomes sheepishly tells me later that he's glad I don't speak better Portuguese.

A local *parkour* group had been Gomes' idea back in 2008 when he was working for an ad agency in nearby Brasilia. He thought it would be a good distraction for a small satellite town that had little except cushy government jobs and the temptation to fall into the drug trade. Gama had gone from slum to merely poor to middle class since Gomes was a child, but happiness was still getting a new car every year and being able to afford cable TV. According to Gomes, there were only two ways to do that: government cronyism or selling drugs.

When Gomes moved to São Paulo to start boo-box, his online advertising company, 50 kids were in the *parkour* group. Since he left, few have stayed clean. The streets may have been paved and the houses may have gone from wood to brick, but some things in Gama haven't changed.

Gomes' future didn't always look so promising. He dropped out of college because he was bored, and he leveraged some experience building Web sites for small businesses into a trainee job at an ad agency in Brasilia. He was shocked at the budgets multinationals would spend to develop simple Web sites he'd been building for years on the cheap. By 19, he was the head of the interactive division.

He started experimenting with new ad formats, and one got the attention of bloggers in Silicon Valley. It was a box that bloggers could embed into stories about products that would, with one click, take you to a site to buy that product. TechCrunch,* the blog that wrote about all those social media companies Gomes loved, called boo-box potential acquisition bait by an Amazon or eBay, and Gomes—who never thought the life of an entrepreneur was an option for him—was floored. Eric Acher, a São Paulo VC, saw the post and cold-called Gomes. "After one conversation I invested in him," Acher says. It was less the idea, which at the time was just a novel product. It was Gomes. There was something about him.

---

*Sarah Lacy is currently the editor-at-large for TechCrunch.

Gomes' uncle—the one who used to smuggle computers until he opened a computer store—is the closest example Gomes had in his life of an entrepreneur, but even he can't understand this new high-growth world in which Gomes lives.

"He gave you $300,000? For what?" his uncle said, incredulous about the first round of venture funding.

"For my company," Gomes said.

"What company?" his uncle protested. "You have no company!"

But in a short time, Gomes has more than 20 employees and a bigger company than his uncle ever did.

I asked Gomes' mother if she was surprised that he'd gotten out of Gama. We were sitting in the crowded two-room house that a young Gomes had to live in alone for a few years while his parents made money working hundreds a miles away in the Amazon, close to the Bolivian border. She was giving a makeover to her niece, who was going to a 1960s-themed church dance later that night, drawing long sweeping lines on her eyelids with some old liquid eyeliner. The young niece's baby cried in a cousin's arms in the corner. His mother paused from the makeover, looked at Gomes, smiled, and told me she wasn't surprised. She, too, always thought there was something special about him. "It's his brother I'm worried about," she added with a laugh. It's clear Gomes feels that mix of guilt, pride, and comfort when visiting his hometown. He says if boo-box makes it big, he's going to pay for his parents to work as missionaries in the Amazon for a year.

Boo-box is an online ad network that aggregates ad space on thousands of blogs, Twitter streams, video feeds, and any other online media, offering advertisers a huge base of Brazilian social media eyeballs, spread across thousands of sites. From a Silicon Valley perspective, this business has been done to death, but it's still novel in Brazil's $2 billion a year online advertising market, and boo-box takes a very creative approach, constantly experimenting with new formats advertisers might buy. Brazil has about 25 percent Internet penetration, so there's a lot of room for growth.

Many Americans see advertising as the annoying trade-off for consuming free media, but Gomes calls it the very cornerstone of capitalism. He thinks that anyone posting anything online should have the right to make money on it—even if it's just pennies for Tweets. In Silicon Valley, many people find the idea of hawking goods to your friends over Twitter as mercenary and sleazy. But seeing the life the Internet lifted Gomes out of, it becomes something different. For Gomes, it's about empowering anyone with a Web connection to find his or her own way out.

I'd expected for slum-based entrepreneurship to be a big theme in this book. There is something about having nothing to lose that makes you take more risk, makes you hungrier. Entrepreneurship is about changing the status quo, and the most disenfranchised would logically be the ones pushing hardest for that change. But traveling the developing world—places ripped apart by colonialism, violence, and political oppression that are now surging toward uneven, rapid growth—is a humbling lesson in the different types of poverty in the world.

While there's little that can compare to the unmet human needs in an Indian slum, there's also little that can compare to the violence of a Rio *favela*. The number of homicides qualifies it as a civil war zone between drug kingpins and often-corrupt police officers. Brazil has 3 percent of the world's population and yet 11 percent of the homicides, most of which happen in *favelas*.[5]

Life in an Indian slum and a Brazilian *favela* are a daily fight for survival, but the fight is very different. In India, it's a fight for basic human needs like food, water, and protection from disease. In Brazil, the infrastructure and living conditions in *favelas* are far better, but the daily struggle is avoiding bullets. There is something about the former situation that makes the idea of starting a company so far off that it's a laughable, naïve suggestion. But there's something about Brazil's *favelas* where the right ambitious, cocky, or brilliant kid can still dream big and can still find his or her way out. As Brazil's Web penetration increases, that way out is increasingly the Internet.

Narayana Murthy, of Infosys, described the difference between China and India by saying China chose to give its people economic freedom before political freedom, whereas India had given people political freedom before economic freedom. It remains to be seen which country—if either—will make good on both. But by contrast, right now Brazil is experiencing a greater period of political freedom and economic freedom than it ever has before. Brazil's big problem is safety—an issue India and China largely don't have.

When Chase invested in Argentinian-born entrepreneur Wences Casares' online brokerage he moved to São Paulo to work with them for several months. He was told to cancel his meetings for a full day of security training. It included an evasive driving simulation, where Casares had to wreck several expensive cars to get away. At the end of the training, Chase's head of security gave Casares $2,000 in cash and a phone number and told him to carry both with him everywhere. If all else failed, the security chief said, give the kidnappers the cash and tell them to call the number to get more. Every day, when Casares went to work, he'd make sure he had his wallet, his keys, his phone, and the $2,000 in cash. It became so routine that it wasn't until he finished the assignment and flew back to his home in Silicon Valley that he realized he still had Chase's cash is his pocket.

At first, Casares thought the security precautions were absurd and unnecessary. He knew life and business in South America as well as anyone. He grew up on a sheep farm in Patagonia, and dropped out of college to build his online brokerage, Patagon. He would eventually sell it $750 million, and follow that up with three-years of sailing around the world, and then starting and selling several more banks in Europe and Latin America. He wasn't one to live his life in fear. Then one day in São Paulo, his car was followed and his pulse started racing. He got away, but the experience changed how he thought of Brazil, a country he loved, but one he wasn't sure he could live in now, especially as the father of three children.

With the pressure of the World Cup and Olympics mounting, finally Rio—the epicenter of the problem—is addressing the violence and poverty that have long plagued the shanty buildings crowding its cliffs and hillsides. The city is embarking on a plan called "Pacification," where newly trained, SWAT-style cops take each *favela* back, one-by-one, driving out the drug dealers by any means necessary. Being new to the force, these officers have a clean slate with the residents of the *favela*. They are able to gain their trust and continue protecting the neighborhood after pacification.

Only eight *favelas* had been pacified at the time of publication, but the difference inside them is staggering. Before there was a palpable fear that pervaded everyday life—fear of getting caught in a crossfire, fear of your kids falling into the drug trade, fear of being confused for a snitch, fear that the drug lord in your neighborhood may snap at any moment. With that low-level, constant anxiety gone, suddenly *favela* residents can be part of Rio. People have gone to the beach for the first time. People have had a cab drop them off at their houses for the first time. People have had pizza delivered for the first time. And many of the wealthier residents have gone into a *favela* for the first time.

One *favela* was so dangerous that city trash collectors wouldn't enter it, and the accumulated filth lead to a severe rat infestation. Babies were covered with bites, frequently getting diseases as a result. Some kids in the *favela* videotaped it and posted the footage on YouTube, using the equipment of a nonprofit CDI, which has built 800 computer labs throughout Brazil's roughest neighborhoods. Horrified and publicly shamed, the city came in and cleaned things up. But without pacification, services like these can't be maintained.

Optimism aside, many are skeptical that the pacification will last. "This is the best I've seen the community in a long time, but I'm still scared," said Nivea Mendes of the pacified *favela* Babilonia. "Very few people trust the government. They are just out for an election." Even though they're physically gone, the drug dealers still have power in these neighborhoods. No one wants to embrace the police too much, lest the city loosen its resolve and the drug lords return.

There are other issues with pacification, too. Critics say the crime isn't eradicated; it just moves outside of Rio's hillsides, creating more problems for the countryside and smaller cities. Another issue is that it takes time. Keeping the peace requires constant vigilance. And, strangely, it hurts small businesses at first, by shoving the richest people—the criminals—out of the *favela*, creating a need for a new livelihood for merchants and survival-level entrepreneurs in these neighborhoods. But overall, residents are still relieved that the city is finally doing something. The assumption had been that Rio would solve the problem during the World Cup and Olympics by just asking the drug dealers how much they wanted for a temporary cease-fire and paying it.

Many entrepreneurs—like Gomes—didn't wait for pacification to get out. They are the exceptions, but there's a generation of slum-born entrepreneurs in Brazil who one by one used whatever they had to build a company and a new life. It's increasingly a third option to the violent but powerful drug trade and life as an evangelical Christian with a low-paying, virtuous job. For Gomes it was the Internet. For Zica Assis it was her problematic, frizzy hair.

Assis blamed her hair for everything—getting teased at school, not having a boyfriend, even for not getting the right job. When she was little she used to tie a towel around her head and go around the house swinging it like it was the long, luxurious hair she'd always wanted.

Assis went to beauty school, but at the time there was a high tax on imports, and buying anything like a relaxer was out of her reach. No one targeted women with curly hair in the slums because the assumption was they were too poor to afford treatments. Stylists would just comb the hair, making it frizz more. Assis spent nearly 10 years in her garage concocting different products and testing them on her younger brother, Rogerio. After all, she could just buzz his hair off if things went too badly. A few times his hair fell out completely.

Finally, she opened the first salon, called Beleza Natural, with a friend Leila Velez, who would later marry Rogerio. The salon was staffed by six people in a space that was just 30 square meters. More than 100 people lined up the first day for treatments. They charged $15 a head, and people would wait as long as 12 hours to get their hair done by Assis and Velez. In a country where some 70 percent of the population has Assis's mixed-race genetics and naturally curly hair, Beleza Natural didn't need to advertise.

As demand grew, the three studied companies like McDonald's for the way they used assembly-line processes and Disney for how they moved people through lines. The biggest problem wasn't bringing in customers—it was processing all those heads of hair in an efficient way. The company does about $55 million in annual revenues today and relaxes and styles about 80,000 Brazilians per month.

So far most of the salons are in Rio, but Beleza Natural wants to expand more broadly in the country. Assis's ultimate dream is opening salons in Africa. But working capital, staffing, and managing growth are daunting challenges. "We always thought we'd just see if we could get a little bit bigger, but today we have a huge vision," says her brother Rogerio, who has graduated from style guinea pig to the company's vice president. "But it's hard, because we are big enough we don't get government grants but still too small for other kinds of financing. Any wrong move can break the company." Still, growing up as a young girl in a poor neighborhood and being teased for her hair, these are problems Assis never thought she'd have.

As these two segregated halves of the city slowly come together, it's not just poor entrepreneurs who are benefiting. Compared to Gomes or Assis, restaurateurs Mario Chady and Eduardo Ourivio have had charmed lives, living in big houses, partying late at night in the clubs, and surfing on Rio's stunning beaches every morning.

"The key is to get a little bit of Rio into your life every day," says Chady from a party on a yacht overlooking the twinkling city lights, as samba music thumps in the background. But Chady and Ourivio's success hasn't come by selling to wealthy peers; it's come from painstakingly building a fast-food empire that has grown along with Brazil's aspirational lower-middle class.

It hasn't been easy. The effort has been plagued with false starts, crushing debt, and for both Ourivio and Chady serious health problems caused by the stress. But today the company, Spoleto, operates more than 250 cheap-but-fresh pasta restaurants, along with Brazil's Domino's Pizza franchise and a recent acquisition of popular fast-food sushi chain, Koni. The company is doing more than $100 million in annual revenues and is the fourth largest fast-food company in the country; the first three are all foreign-owned or local franchises of foreign brands like KFC and McDonald's. "In three years we will double the size of this company without what I call any 'business Viagra,'" Ourivio says, referring to private equity or other acquisitions.

In finance, a company called Crivo, has developed a way to do lightning-fast, three-second credit checks that could open up a world of debt for this burgeoning middle class. There's nothing like a FICO score in Brazil, so, in the past, credit decisions were made based on negative data and positive data. In other words, a person is either good or bad in the bank's eyes. There's little record for positive data in Brazil, because the wealthiest people don't want public records showing how much they paid for a house or a car for security reasons. That only leaves negative data. So if there's no information about someone, it's assumed he or she is a good credit risk. But with one missed payment, he or she becomes a "dirty name."

It's an obviously flawed system, says Crivo's CEO Daniel Turini. Many good credit risks have missed a payment before, and it's a huge assumption to make that someone with no credit history would be a safe credit risk. Crivo solves the problem with an army of servers that pull information from a variety of sources, including things like utility records to verify an applicant's address or ensuring that their phone number doesn't just go to a payphone. Just a single piece of basic information can eliminate fraud, Turini says.

There are clear ripple effects if Crivo does well. More people getting credit cards helps grow spending and ecommerce, more small businesses can get loans, and more working families can buy houses. Many people in the United States may have overdone it in the last decade, but smart access to debt isn't all bad.

⌒∞⌒

Over the first 20 years of this century, per capita incomes in Brazil will increase by 50 percent, which is small only compared to China where they are tripling and India and Russia where they are doubling.[6] Considering these four countries make up more than 40 percent of the world population, this change is undoubtedly a good thing when it comes to human rights. It's also a good thing politically, because comfortable middle classes are far less likely to become radicalized. And as we've seen in China, India, and Brazil, increased income creates a host of new business opportunities for scrappy local entrepreneurs.

But with this surge in relative affluence, more people are able to afford protein-rich diets and electricity-powered lifestyles, and that is causing huge spikes in the commodity markets. This creates challenges for Brazil, but it also creates huge opportunities. Increasingly, Brazil is the country feeding the rest of the emerging world. While Russia is the third largest importer of agricultural products in the world, Brazil is the fourth largest exporter. That means as prices and demand continue to rise, an emerging market like Russia will have to pay more, but a market like Brazil is sitting on a potential gold mine.

As for energy, Brazil not only discovered a huge trove of oil in 2007, but it is also one of the most ambitious countries when it comes to producing renewable energy like hydroelectric power, sugar cane ethanol, and other biofuels. Brazil runs on 80 percent hydroelectric power, and more than 90 percent of the new cars sold in Brazil can run on gas or ethanol.[7]

Brazil's best domestic opportunity may be building out consumer products and services for its burgeoning middle class, but its best global opportunity is reinventing old industries like agriculture and energy that the world as a whole is desperate to remake. In a sector with this much demand, this much spending, and this much need for innovation, there are plenty of juicy niches for smart entrepreneurs.

Heraldo Negri has found a particularly icky one. Negri loves bugs. I mean, he really loves bugs. Negri is like that kid you knew who used to spend recess digging up worms, wearing cicada shells as accessories, and putting spiders on pretty girls' chairs—only he never grew out of it. Negri has photo albums full of pictures of bugs he started taking as a teen. He even has a side business self-publishing books full of pictures of every bug he's ever met in various stages of life. He insisted on sending me home with several copies of these books, saying, "Your husband is going to love these!" as if he's sneaking me a stack of *Playboy* magazines.

Appropriately, Negri's company is called Bug, and that's what it makes—millions of bugs. Specifically, he breeds wasps that kill the caterpillars that plague Brazil's most lucrative crops. Twenty-five years after the first field tests of genetically modified organisms, many are already becoming less pest-resistant. Meanwhile, overuse of chemical pesticides have killed many of the pests' natural predators, so when the caterpillars come back, they've got an unfair advantage over the plants. Bug is fighting back using not technology, but nature.

Negri takes very good care of his special little friends. There's a cook on staff who serves up a peanut-buttery concoction they feed on, and he keeps every room at the optimal temperature for gestation. Negri harvests the wasps' eggs and sells them to farmers. The eggs hatch, and the baby wasps burrow into the caterpillar's eggs like a parasite. When those eggs hatch, the joke is on the caterpillar—there's nothing but more baby wasps inside. It's gross, but organic, which increasingly fetches higher prices in the global market.

Bug's real innovation is the adhesive that glues the eggs between two sheets of cardboard without harming them. Farmers get stacks of these cardboard sheets and break apart perforated squares, distributing them throughout a field. Hundreds of eggs—each about the size of a finely ground speck of pepper—are inside each thumbprint-size square. The cardboard keeps them safe until they hatch. Then, they fly out through the perforations and do what nature programmed them to do.

Like Beleza Natural, Bug's problem was never generating demand, it was scaling the business to meet all that demand. The company was a risky investment in a country that doesn't take a ton of venture risk. The technology was there, but several VCs walked away from negotiations because the company didn't yet have certification to sell its bugs to farmers. An investor named Francisco Jardim took the risk when no one else would. Now that Bug is one of the only companies that have this certification, it's one of the most promising companies in Jardim's portfolio. Brazil is the largest pesticide user in the world, recently overtaking the United States. Certification takes several years, and tellingly, some big multinationals and other upstarts have recently started to apply, Jardim says. Meanwhile, Bug is upgrading into better, larger bug-growing facilities—a step up from the motley series of houses and the old supermarket where it has been raising its bugs.

⌘

While Bug seeks to profit from Brazil's agricultural boom, several hundred miles north in the Amazon basin, another unlikely start-up is seeking to profit off one of Brazil's largest renewable energy projects. It's called BS Construtora, it has never raised a penny of outside funding, and it's already generating more than $100 million in annual revenues.

After several hours in the air and several more in a pickup truck, the rain forest opens up to something that looks like the set of a movie—a cross between the suburban opening of *Edward Scissorhands* and the eerie village where The Others live on the TV show "Lost." Hundreds of orange, yellow, and green houses dot newly poured asphalt streets, curving in a familiar pattern of suburban cul-de-sacs. Modern-day water, sewage systems, power, phone lines, and even Internet access run to each house. The sky is blue with fluffy white clouds, making the pastel boxes filling this valley all the more otherworldly and surreal.

This is just the beginning of a $120 million, 1,600-house village that BS Construtora is building, complete with three schools, a basketball court, a mall, a fire department, a police station, a hotel, restaurants, bars, a golf course, and other staples of modern suburban life. I thought India's mosquito-free Hiware Bazar was modern and clean. This village is downright sterile, with the good and the bad that description implies.

The village is part of a major multibillion-dollar hydroelectric project that will flood an area of the jungle in exchange for providing Northern Brazil with cheap, sustainable energy. And the village will be an odd mix of workers and supervisors hired to build and maintain the dam, and hundreds of people who will be displaced when the dam is built and water floods the jungle. Most of the workers come from the cities. Most of the jungle residents have never lived in a house. Talk about culture clash. It's a barrage of potential first-world and third-world problems colliding in one eerie, pastel-colored village of the dam.

BS Construtora isn't some multinational giant like the U.S. companies that are rebuilding war-torn areas of the Middle East. It's a startup. It won this plum job through innovation, not heft or government connections. Specifically, BS Construtora can do what many other prefab housing vendors can't; it can build an entire house from start to finish in one day. It does this by pouring concrete into molds that make one whole room at a time, not one wall at a time. The formula has to be exactly right for them to come out in one piece, so a chemist tests each batch. Then the rooms—with holes left for electrical and plumbing—are put together to make a house. BS Construtora's founder Sidnei Borges dos Santos got the idea from looking at a shoebox and turning it upside down.

Borges dos Santos was the son of a subsistence farmer, and he attended school for only four years before he had to quit and help his father out on the farm. His father worried that he was trapping his son in a dreary hand-to-mouth life, but Borges dos Santos wasn't about to let that happen. The inequality of rural Brazilian life infuriated him even as a child. He'd go to friends' houses who had meat and soft drinks every night. For Borges dos Santos' family, these were things for holidays. Even at a young age, he wanted more.

In his early teens, Borges dos Santos sold ice cream in the summers and cut lawns in the winter. He discovered that he had a knack for sales, doing little things like waking up earlier than his competitors and taking special care with his appearance. "I bathed three times more than other kids," he says proudly. He'd do extra services like weeding the flower gardens and taking out the trash, and his business grew.

In his mid-teens, he got a job on a construction site as the guy who mixed the brick mortar, several rungs below the bricklayer. His family relied on his income more, and it drove him to wake up earlier and work harder. He began to climb the construction ladder.

In his late-teens, he decided to go back to school, but he was distracted when he overheard his teacher talking about building a new pigsty. Borges dos Santos went to his teacher's house every day and begged for the tiny 1,500-square-meter construction job. More jobs followed, and he hired his father as his first employee and bought a motorcycle and an old, beat-up Brazilian-made car with his first checks.

A bigger life change came when he started going to church—not because, like Marco Gomes, he fell in love with religion, but because he fell in love with Eliane, the preacher's daughter. When her family moved, Borges dos Santos didn't think twice; he moved, too, and his family came with him. Never mind that back then, Eliane wanted nothing to do with him.

Several years, towns, and construction jobs later, personal tragedy struck: Eliane's brother—also Borges dos Santos' best friend—died in a car accident. Through their grief, he finally won her over, and within a year they were engaged. And then, financial tragedy struck: The week he was supposed to get married, Borges dos Santos bounced 600 checks. He hadn't exactly been a monk while he was waiting for Eliane. He was making an impressive $200,000 a year, but he was $300,000 in debt. He'd done reckless things like swap cars 20 times in one year. He calls it a mix between "passion, craziness, and finally having money for the first time." "There were 40,000 people in this city, and I'd bounced at least two checks at each place," he says.

To his surprise, the woman he'd fought for so many years to marry didn't leave him, but it was a brutal time. No one wanted to hire Borges dos Santos. He would have to wait until after midnight to come home, because debtors were waiting on him. His oldest employee, Salvador, had a family, and Borges dos Santos couldn't pay him the back salary he owed him. The shame was crushing. "I wanted to die," he says. "I knew he had to feed his family, but I didn't have any money."

Finally, someone in town gave Borges dos Santos a $50,000 contract to build a silo. When the client handed him a $30,000 check for supplies, Borges dos Santos' hands were shaking. He gave the man his word of honor that he wouldn't use any of the money to repay his debts until the silo was done. Eliane got the supplies for 30 percent less than Borges dos Santos ever had, so his margins were much better. He built the silo, and together they slowly rebuilt the company, their finances, and their lives.

Several years later, Borges dos Santos found himself bidding on a huge contract that included pigsties, factories, and 1,500 houses. He knew nothing about house construction, and this was when he had his shoebox inspiration. He pitched it, with no idea if it would actually work. "Son of a bitch, why didn't I think of that?" the client said and gave him the deal.

BS Construtora is pushing for larger growth and wants to go public in the next few years, but this is a tough business with thin margins. Deals to build 1,500 houses at a time don't come along every day, and building homes to sell to Brazil's turbulent, emerging middle class is a boom-and-bust business. BS Construtora refuses to compete on cost; it competes on quality and speed, so other companies can underbid and win deals.

But for now it is one of those rare companies that has all the right ingredients. It's solving a huge problem for its country and the emerging world at large. It has a proven concept, nine-figure revenues, a track record for delivering huge projects, a visionary founder, and now, a professional Stanford-trained CEO, a 30-something Brazilian returnee named Marcelo Miranda. And like India's low-cost telecom base station company VNL, BS Construtora may have come up with an innovative way to solve a problem that even poorer countries are grappling with, giving huge populations of displaced people a place to call home.

Brazil may not have grown as fast as China or India in the last 10 years, but a network effect is happening slowly but surely as the country stabilizes. It's not any one sector that makes Brazil an emerging market; it's the interplay between the government's efforts to eradicate poverty and violence, tech companies like Crivo that facilitate consumer lending, companies like BS Construtora that can quickly build new, modern neighborhoods, and other consumer goods that fill in the needs of a new ascendant middle class, while commodities and cleantech could be the sexy, disruptive growth industry that the computer was in the United States in the late 20th century. A deeply divided nation—whether between slum and mansion or between city and country—is starting to become whole.

❧

São Paulo is the business hub of Brazil, but nearby Rio is the most emblematic of the country's natural beauty, its passion, and its divisive violence. As Brazil's prestige has grown in the eyes of Wall Street and multinationals in recent years, São Paulo has finally gotten its chance to gloat over the more glamorous city to the East. A common joke is that the huge Christ statue in Rio isn't waiting with arms outstretched to embrace his followers—he's waiting to applaud when the beach bums of Rio finally start working.

But in 2016, Rio will have its Beijing moment when it hosts the Olympic games. While the World Cup has been in South America many times, this is the first time the forgotten continent will host the Olympics. If Rio can keep a lid on the violence, the city and country will shine. Brazil's image in the world is no small issue for the country's entrepreneurs. While Brazil has gained attention from Wall Street investors who are interested in taking former government-owned behemoths private or lending money to the central government, very few early-stage venture capitalists invest in Brazil. Considering how much money flows to China and India, it's surprising.

Silicon Valley investors give two reasons for this reluctance. The first is violence. Wealthy Silicon Valley investors have a lot of countries where they can spend their money, so they need a compelling reason to risk a kidnapping to do it in Brazil. And so far, the returns haven't been there to make it compelling the way they have been in China. The other reason has to do with relationships. Venture capital has long been a local business, and the only way it works globally is through personal relationships. While investment in China has soared because of the opportunity and the returns, investment in India has soared mostly because of these relationships. People in Silicon Valley believe in India.

The closest there is to a high-profile Brazil entrepreneur in the Valley is Casares, who is from Argentina originally. It's partially a result of Brazil's isolationist streak. A lot of people don't want to leave. And increasingly, immigration issues in the United States are driving the people who do come to the Valley back home. BS Construtora's CEO Miranda was finishing up a mini-MBA at Stanford about the time America headed into recession. He was told by American companies that it "wasn't a good time" to hire foreigners; meanwhile, he got more than a dozen high-profile offers in Brazil.

Without greater personal ties, Silicon Valley venture capital will never flood into Brazil, and Brazil isn't the only one vying for those dollars. Chile has an aggressive program to attract Silicon Valley talent and capital, and several social gaming companies have been expanding operations in Argentina, a country that in the 1990s got more venture capital than anywhere else in Latin America.

That's bad news for entrepreneurs like Gomes, who are trying to start Silicon Valley–style Internet companies and could use the cash and connections, but it's hardly disastrous. Venture capital can be a catalyst, but as companies in this chapter prove, it isn't everything. Gomes is building his Internet company with local funding, as is Bug. Spoleto's founders built a 250-plus chain restaurant company with debt and working capital. Beleza Natural has built a $50 million revenue beauty business that global brands missed and thousands of Brazilian women can't live without. BS Construtora has bootstrapped what should be an unbootstrapable idea to a point where it's winning $120 million contracts at a time. The United States made itself a superpower through its entrepreneurial spirit, and that same self-reliance is propelling the best sectors of Brazil's nascent entrepreneur ecosystem some 50 years later.

There are even some advantages to being ignored by the West. Just ask entrepreneurs in Indonesia, a country larger than Brazil that is so ignored it doesn't even make it into Goldman Sach's BRIC moniker. And Indonesia is a country where the legacy effects of colonization on entrepreneurship loom even larger.

Indonesia

9

The Emerging World's Big Secret

When Ciputra was in his late twenties, he sent a letter to Walt Disney. He'd just gotten a plot of beach property from Indonesia's charismatic and debaucherous first president, Sukarno, who was hell-bent on transforming Jakarta into a modern capital city even if it bankrupted the rest of the nation in the process. Ciputra—who, like many Indonesians of his era, mostly goes by just one name—was fresh out of architecture school, and he had traveled to Disneyland once. He didn't care so much about the rides, the beloved characters walking around, or the songs and parades, but he fell in love with Disney's sense of architecture. He was writing to Disney to suggest that the two men partner on a Disney-style theme park in Jakarta.

Disney wrote back a two-sentence letter telling the young Ciputra that he was not going to open a Disneyland in Jakarta, and he strongly advised him not to use the name. Ciputra wasn't so much angry as he was confused. He saw the opportunity so clearly. How could a man like Disney not see it? Determined to prove he was right, he built an amusement park anyway on the Ancol property. Then he built out the waterfront. Then he added an artist village. Then he added restaurants, hotels, golf courses, and houses. And then he added a Sea World. Ancol is now the fourth most-attended amusement park in the world, following Disney World, Disneyland, and Tokyo Disney. It's even ahead of Disneyland Paris. But Ciputra, now in his eighties, isn't smug. He's not going to gloat. Well, at least not until Ancol reaches number one.

This story sums up the foreign investment catch-22 of Indonesia. It's a nation of 240 million people—the fourth largest in the world—and it is mostly unserved by Western multinationals. It's also a nation rich with natural resources, including oil and minerals, and a climate that can grow more than 30,000 spices, coffee, rice, and other valuable commodities. Yet, as Israel proves, population and natural resources aren't everything. For all its empirical assets, Indonesia's gross domestic product is just $510 billion; compare that to Mexico's $847 billion with less than half of the population and Singapore's $181 billion with a population of less than 5 million people. Indonesia is a giant that's economically still asleep. Pick your favorite reason why: Indonesia has been one of the most dominated, unstable, tragedy-stricken countries of the 20th century.

Between the Dutch and the Japanese, Indonesia was colonized for some 350 years. And it was a brutal occupation where the native Indonesians worked like slaves, while the great riches of the country were plundered. There was no building an educational system. There was no establishing a rule of law. There was no training the Indonesians for better jobs. The Dutch occupiers didn't want them to rise up. Only the Chinese immigrants were allowed to start companies, as the Dutch anointed the Chinese as the local mercantile class, not the native Indonesians. This left a lasting impact on the country. Indonesians may be the only people who envy 20th-century China. "They were only held down by communism for 50 years," Ciputra says. "We were held down for 350 years."

After independence, Indonesia fell into the trend of dictators, first Sukarno, who flirted with communism, and then Suharto, who had been Sukarno's number two but seized power in a turbulent coup, blaming it on Indonesia's communist party and causing a violent backlash throughout the country. Suharto talked a good game to the West by vehemently opposing communism during the Cold War, and the United States gave him a lot of aid and diplomatic support in return.

Under Suharto, Indonesia posted three decades of strong economic growth, but unfortunately all of that was undone in the disastrous late 1990s Asian financial crisis. Every company and crony under Suharto was allowed to operate a bank, leading to an orgy of interlending that made the financial crash especially hard on Indonesia.[1] "Not only did regular godfathers have banks, Suharto's children had banks, Suharto's bribe-gathering foundations owned banks and different factions of the military had banks," according to Joe Studwell's book *Asian Godfathers*.[2]

Things got worse as the banks began to collapse, and the Indonesian government lent billions to tycoons who moved most of that money to Singapore, leaving the government with a hodgepodge of assets worth nothing close to their paper value.[3] *Time Asia* estimated the Suhartos' family fortune to be $15 billion, and he was accused of misappropriation of funds, but he never stood trial because of his declining health. As the Indonesian rupiah and the Jakarta stock exchange plummeted in value and riots broke out throughout the country, it was clear just how fragile Indonesia's so-called economic and political stability were.[4] It was one of the most devastated countries in a wildly devastating crisis.

Finally, after a bloody student demonstration in 1998, Suharto was forced to resign. Indonesia was technically a democracy, but a highly unstable one that had a different president every year until 2001. It wasn't until the current president, Susilo Bambang Yudhoyono—known as "SBY"—was elected that a president in Indonesia served a full, democratically elected term. SBY has said all the right things. He ran based on accountability, strengthening Indonesia's economy through business-friendly changes in regulations and labor laws, and rooting out the corruption and nepotism in government. But SBY was a general under Suharto, and concern lingers that he may have a yet-unseen dark side.[5]

In the early 2000s, the West was becoming infatuated with emerging economies and Indonesia was regaining its economic and political footing, when it was hit with the 2004 Indian Ocean tsunami, one of the most devastating natural disasters in history, triggered by the second largest earthquake ever measured. Hundreds of thousands of people died, one-third of whom were children. In addition to all these political, economic, and natural disasters, there's the West's trepidation about doing business with the largest Muslim nation on earth in a post-9/11 world. Looking at all of this, the great mystery of why Indonesia is so ignored by investors starts to become clear. It's even a difficult country to understand geographically, because it's a nation of 17,000 islands, many of which are uninhabited. It took 30 years for the international community to even grant the waters between the islands as sovereign territory.

Yet, even the sharpest critics of Indonesia have noted the progress the country has made. A lot of that has to do with SBY, whose approval rating has topped 70 percent[6] and who won his second election in a landslide. Economic growth has been roughly 6 percent per year, inflation has been tamed, and he's streamlined Indonesia's bureaucracy.[7] The risk of a coup still looms, but as long as the president remains this popular, Indonesia is seen as far more stable than its neighbors like the Philippines or Thailand.[8]

Ciputra has lived through all of this. He was born during the Dutch colonial days when only Chinese families like his were allowed to start companies. His father, a shopkeeper, was captured and killed during the Japanese occupation. Sukarno gave him his first plot of land and opportunity. During the anti-Chinese backlash in the waning Suharto regime, Ciputra spent days holed up in his mansion terrified that his malls would be destroyed along with so many others. He sat by the phone, horror-struck at what was happening to his country, waiting for the inevitable call. He made a deal with God that if his companies and his family were spared, he would be a better person. When Indonesia's currency and banking system collapsed in the late 1990s, Ciputra was one of only a few moguls who didn't move his money to Singapore. He was horribly in debt, but he stuck it out and made the money back—and more. He's cagey about anyone knowing his net worth, but he's easily one of the richest men in Indonesia, and his three development companies pay in excess of $100 million in taxes every year. His family may be ethnically Chinese, but Ciputra is an Indonesian.

Today he is determined to give every last dollar and breath to build one last grand project—an entrepreneurial class in Indonesia that he believes will transform the country. This idea started on his 70th birthday. Ciputra was reflecting on his own life and the leap he made from a poor, orphaned kid in an island village of a turbulent nation to a billionaire real estate mogul. It occurred to him that all Indonesia needed were more Ciputras to make a similar quantum leap as a country.

When Ciputra graduated, he started a consulting company for other developers. But he hated not having control over the projects, so he started developing buildings himself, before moving on to whole blocks, and then mini-cities. In all, Ciputra has developed 50 cities spanning 25,000 hectares. The capital of Jakarta quite literally has his fingerprints all over it. When I asked what his favorite development is, he answered "whichever one I am working on now." And now, he is working on rebuilding Indonesia.

Only someone bored with building cities could dream up a plan to rebuild an entire 240-million-person nation.

Ciputra's team did a good deal of market research on how Indonesian entrepreneurs compare to other countries. He counted about 400,000 high-growth entrepreneurs in Indonesia—less than .08 percent of the population. That compares to 13 percent of the population in the United States, 1.2 percent of the population in India, and 2 percent of the population of Malaysia. But the most galling statistic to Ciputra is that entrepreneurs make up a whopping 7 percent of Singapore's population. "Indonesia has minerals, coal, oil, and what does Singapore have? Nothing! And they make fifteen times our income," he says. He argues that Indonesia's natural resources are a blessing and a curse. Great entrepreneurs build from "nothing but their thoughts." "The only way we've made any money is from the stomachs of our earth," he says. "It's the curse of having oil. It's the Dutch disease."

Ciputra thinks his goal is reasonable: 25 years from now he wants 2 percent of Indonesia's population to be high-growth entrepreneurs. The problem, he says, is education. Indonesians are highly educated for a poor nation, but in the wrong things, Ciputra says. People go to school because they want a government job. No one is trained to think they can create jobs. "It's the mindset we need to change," Ciputra says over and over again. He tightly closes his eyes as he emphasizes each word, pointing to his forehead with his long, rounded nails.

In 2006, he invested $10 million in a university to teach entrepreneurship, and in 2010, it graduated its first class of 166 students. More than 100 of them had already started businesses. These students take all the regular college classes four days a week, but on Wednesdays they study anything an entrepreneur would need to know—from case studies to basic business management. But he's also trying to teach them something more intangible than that. Posters hang in the school that list Ciputra's seven essential entrepreneurial characteristics: Passion, Independent, Market Sensitivity,

Creative & Innovative, Calculated Risk-Taker, Highly Ethical Standard, Persistent. Ciputra told them in his opening lecture to leave if they wanted to work for someone else. He thinks it would be a sign of success if people started dropping out of his college to start companies. It would mean they don't need the security blanket of a government-certified education anymore.

Ciputra is planning to invest another $10 million on a similar university in Jakarta in the next few years. But even that's not enough to change a nation, he says. He wanted to find a way to reach every student, so he developed a five-day course to train teachers from universities throughout Indonesia to teach entrepreneurship. The so-called Training of Trainers program has trained more than 2,000 teachers from more than 350 universities to date. Still not satisfied he was having enough impact, he asked the Ewing Marion Kauffman Foundation to help him to make the program stronger.* Ciputra wanted to learn how the United States gets a stunning 13 percent of its population to be high-growth entrepreneurs. He and the Kauffman Foundation developed a Global Faculty Visitors Program, where more than a dozen lecturers from Indonesia spend six months seeing what works in Boston, Silicon Valley, and other hot spots in the United States. Ciputra dropped another $9 million on that program.

Ciputra staunchly disagrees with those who say entrepreneurs are born and not made. He says it needs to be fostered by parents, schools, or a society. In the United States, society encourages it. He is trying to create a system in Indonesia where schools encourage it. For Ciputra, the encouragement came from his father before he was captured. "Maybe I would be ten times bigger by now, if I'd been encouraged by my environment and training," he says. He points to the fact that the bulk of Indonesian companies are started by ethnically Chinese Indonesians. That was because of Dutch

---

*This book was made possible by a grant from the Kauffman Foundation.

colonialism. "It's not by our genes, it's by discipline," he says. "That can be learned. That is Indonesia's experience."

For three years Ciputra has also been relentlessly lobbying SBY's administration to push a culture of entrepreneurship on a national level. Dino Patti Djalal, the President's spokesperson at the time and now ambassador to the United States, remembers his first conversation with Ciputra and how it "opened (his) eyes." "Entrepreneurship never sounded like anything sexy before, it sounded dull," he says. "Now it was like, *this is it.* This is the magic formula." The next day in a speech, SBY started talking up the importance of Indonesian entrepreneurship, and it has become a cornerstone of his strategy since.

Ciputra rejects the U.S. view that all a government needs to do to spur innovation is get out of the way. "We have to involve the government because we are trying to change the nation entirely," he says. "Our private sector is just here," he says squeezing his thumb and index fingernails together as if he is holding something the size of a mosquito. Ciputra knows that if Indonesia is going to excel, it won't be by mimicking Silicon Valley, Israel, India, or China. It needs to solve the problems endemic to Indonesia and play to its own strengths.

Ciputra is even producing a movie about entrepreneurship to further entice young people. His production crew has shown him a cut of it three times, and it's still not good enough for him. "My people hate me, but I keep sending it back," he says with a mogul-like cackle. "It has to entertain, not just inform."

Indonesia, like so many once-colonized nations, has spent the 20th century fighting for freedom and then fighting to figure out what their nation stands for. Now, it is about building strong economies and making lives better for their citizens. Now, it is the private sector's turn. But for Ciputra, something else is riding on this, too. Indonesia is the largest Muslim nation in the world. Only a small percentage of its population is fundamentalist, but there's an inherent sympathy toward the Arab world, the same way many in the United States are sympathetic toward Israel. Ciputra sees entrepreneurship as the best way for Indonesia to keep its Muslim culture moderate. There's nothing like prosperity to keep someone from getting radicalized, he says.

The SBY administration wants a moderating force, too. "Islam needs a facelift in the 21st century," Djalal says. "We can't be afraid of global entrepreneurship, we have to engage with the West." In a 2010 speech to the Muslim leaders, SBY said "Muslims should know in their hearts that the Islamic glory of the 13th century is not coming back." Adds Djalal, "We need to create the right face of Islam for the Western world. It's not the Taliban, and it's not al-Qaeda. We are the new face of Islam."

That's a brave statement. If Indonesia can stick to the ideals of democracy, entrepreneurship, and moderate Islam, it won't stay a forgotten player on the global business and political stage. But for now the fact that many Western companies perceive Indonesia as more radical that it is has created a local opportunity when it comes to the Web and consumer products, like cosmetics.

⚭

There is nothing subtle about Martha Tilaar's office. Heavily perfumed and air-conditioned, it's an estrogen oasis in this hot, humid country. There are decorative perfume bottles that look like they could house genies, embroidered pillows, satin settees, and paintings of roses and lotus flowers everywhere. On the ceiling above her desk there's a mural of roses flowing out of clouds. Portraits of women are on every wall. The only thing missing is the singing bluebirds.

In the middle of it all is Tilaar, looking immaculate as if she floated down from the sky and landed on a blue satin tuffet. She's wearing an intricately beaded, brightly colored suit-skirt combo. Her black hair is perfectly coiffed in a hair-sprayed bouffant, and her makeup looks like she just applied it moments earlier. "I'm 74 years old," she says proudly. "No facelift and no Botox! Can you imagine if I didn't look good? Who would buy my products?" She exudes a confident, yet appropriately self-deprecating, charm that any finishing school student could learn from.

Tilaar obsesses about the feminine ideal, both personally and professionally. She has spent 40 years building a cosmetics empire in Indonesia, and her guiding light is a huge statue of a Hindu goddess in front of her company's Jakarta headquarters. The goddess has four arms, and Tilaar carefully explains the significance of each. One hand has a rosary, symbolizing that women must be strong in faith and character, she says. The second hand has a sitar, symbolizing the power of communication through charm. "If you play false no one will want to hear you," Tilaar says. The third hand has a leaf used to write on in ancient times. It symbolizes the importance of knowledge and education—the key for a woman's independence, says Tilaar. The fourth hand has a lotus flower, symbolizing a woman's feminity. "A lotus can be planted in a very dirty place, but it can also be planted in a palace," she says. "A woman must adjust to good times and sorrow." To Tilaar, this typifies what it means to be beautiful. "It is not just about a face," she says. "Women must be very soft but must be very strong."

You can see why people call her the Indonesian Oprah, even though she doesn't have a TV show. Through her network of spas and salons, Tilaar has trained and hired thousands of Indonesian women, who might have otherwise been forced to work for subsistence farmer wages—or worse, be sold to Southeast Asia's sex trade. Ten years ago she was in Bali, and a women came running up to her. She was haggard with deep circles under her eyes and gaunt cheekbones. "Ibu Martha! Ibu Martha!" she yelled, coming up to her. "I use your products every day!"

Tilaar was shocked at first, because this woman was hardly the ideal image of beauty, but she was more horrified when she heard the woman's story. She used to be a film star in Jakarta until bad times hit Indonesia. Her family made her come back home, and they sold her into the sex trade to make enough money to feed her siblings. Tilaar thought about this woman day and night for months. She eventually opened a training center in Bali to give other women like her another option.

Going to Tilaar's academy is about more than getting a job; it's almost like going to a finishing school. "I find the pretty girls and I teach them therapies, and to be humble and polite," she says. She tells me of one girl from a poor family who trained with her and became so elegant and polished that she recently married a banker and moved to Malaysia, where she is opening up her own spa. Another woman was a maid until Tilaar took her in and trained her as a hairdresser. She excelled and soon became hairdresser to the first lady of Indonesia. When the Indonesian President and his wife visited the United States, the hairdresser went with them. Tilaar had visited Washington, D.C. before and asked the woman where she stayed. The once uneducated, rural woman answered, "house of Laura Bush." Tilaar—who has pictures of herself with Mother Teresa, Hillary Clinton, and Linda Evangelista—laughs, telling the story, "I stay in hotels, and she stays at the White House!" Growing serious, she adds, "Until my finish I have to help more."

With a focus on female empowerment, Tilaar isn't exactly the kind of mogul many Americans would expect to find in the world's largest Muslim country. But such preconceptions about women in Indonesia are part of the reason she's enjoyed such an untapped market. "All Muslims like to do the makeup," she says. "They all like the spa. They all like beautiful things." When she started her business, only three multinationals were selling cosmetics in Indonesia, and none of them were well designed for the unique climate and culture of the country.

Few products are designed for women who cover themselves head to toe with scarves and live in such extreme heat and humidity. Many women go bald because of the humidity's effects on hair that is kept underneath a scarf all day. And many go grey prematurely, because when their hair doesn't see the sun, the melanin stops working. Younger, more modern Indonesian women want to look paler and more Western. Tilaar has products for all of these specific uses, and they're mostly organic, drawing from the 5 million indigenous herbs and 30,000 spices found on Indonesia's 17,000 islands.

Tilaar spent years hiking out to meet with local shamans to learn indigenous beauty and health treatments. "People would say, 'Look at that crazy woman, what is she doing?'" she says. "But I see it as giving soul to globalization by bringing in the local wisdom." During our interview, I tried to take some medicine for a migraine, and she rushed out of her office, coming back moments later with a steaming hot cup of spicy herbs, telling me to drink it instead.

Tilaar was born frail and sickly in a small village on the island of Java. The doctor told her mother: "You have to be patient with her, she will be a slow learner." Tilaar's brother and sister always got the highest academic ranking in school, and Tilaar was always struggling. Ranking matters more than anything else in Indonesia, because like in India, it's the way to get a good government job and get ahead. One day, Tilaar came running home, yelling, "Mama! I finally have a ranking! I am third from the last in class!" Her mother wasn't amused. She told her, "You will have to use your eyes, face, hands, and feet. You will have to work hard in life."

It was her mother who encouraged Tilaar to be an entrepreneur. She once stole money from her purse to buy some candy. Her mother admonished her and said she would give her money, but she would have to find a way to earn it back. She went to the market, bought up candy and nuts and repackaged them in smaller bags that she sold to her friends for a profit. She sold the mangoes from the tree in her backyard. She made bracelets and necklaces from the dried fruits and spices in her garden. She didn't have brains, so she learned early on to use whatever she did have to get ahead.

In the 1960s, Tilaar went to the United States with her husband, a teacher who had a scholarship at a university. Tilaar had also been a teacher in Indonesia, but she wasn't allowed to work in the United States for visa reasons. So she starting a babysitting business and made more than 10 times her husband's library wages in the first month. Later, she trained to be a beautician. Almost five years later, when the two returned to Indonesia, they got a house close to the ambassadorial residences in Jakarta. Tilaar paid the newsboys to slip flyers into the English-language papers saying she was a beautician trained in the United States and was offering salon services. "I would like to serve you," it read in simple English.

Today, her company operates 48 spas, 40 retail stores, and nine different beauty brands that include more than 5,000 products, ranging in price from $1 to $10. The Martha Tilaar beauty school has had 300,000 students over the years, some taking just a basic class on applying makeup. But her road to success hasn't always been smooth. Her business tanked in the late 1990s financial crisis. She owed a Singapore bank 1 billion rupiahs, which inflated as high as 6 billion. She flew to see the bank's officers and told them she would pay it off if it took her last drop of blood. Today her company does more than $100 million in revenues, having grown 20 percent in 2007, 2008, and 2009. A lot of that is due to her male CEO Hartanto Santosa; Tilaar admits she is more a visionary than a manager.

The two clash from time to time, as Santosa is motivated by business and Tilaar is motivated by cause. Hers is a stubborn idealism. Fifteen years ago, the company acquired a huge tract of land on which Santosa wanted to build a factory. Tilaar insisted it be used for an organic teaching farm instead, quoting her grandmother as saying, "If you are successful using plants you have to replant them." Santosa refused. "This is valuable land," he said. Tilaar broke the stalemate by buying the land from the company herself and planting her farm.

Tilaar also personally bankrolled an annual Miss Indonesia pageant, annoyed that Indonesia wasn't represented in the Miss Universe or Miss World pageants. There is obviously some religious objection to a competition like this in Indonesia. Tilaar says she picked Miss World over Miss Universe because there was a greater emphasis on the talent and Q&A sections, and the girls could wear sarongs during the bathing suit competition.

Tilaar and Ciputra are friends, and not surprisingly they view the plight of Indonesian entrepreneurship through the same lens: Change the mindset and you will unlock a nation of creative problem solvers onto a huge, untapped domestic market. And neither are shy about spending millions of their own money to push the country in that direction.

∞

Interestingly, Ciputra, Tilaar, and the government aren't considering the most logical ally in their quest to create a new generation of entrepreneurs—the Internet. Indonesia has matured from its early 2000s obsession with the now passé social network Friendster to become a Web force, catching the largest Silicon Valley companies off guard with huge swarms of traffic. Obscure Indonesian Awards shows have taken over the chatter on Twitter; Indonesians make up Facebook's second largest audience in the world; and in 2010, Indonesians flocking to see *Iron Man 2* won their first Super Swarm Badge on the location-based game FourSquare—something U.S. Web addicts usually only earn at large technology conferences. Indonesia has the largest Foursquare audience, the second largest Facebook audience, and the most Web users per capita on Twitter of any country in the world. If the American Web audience is rooted in transactions and information, and the Chinese Web audience is rooted in online video and massive multiplayer games, the Indonesian Web audience is all about social networks. E-mail has taken off in Indonesia only recently, mostly because sites like Facebook require an e-mail address to create an account. Little ecommerce is transacted, and the most popular games are those played over social networks.

This social-media-first phenomenon has created a unique Web ecosystem in Indonesia, where offline and online worlds are deeply intertwined, and everything is about facilitating real-world transactions, relationships, and communication. At midnight on a Friday night in Jakarta, teens are packed into gritty, smoke-filled Internet cafés playing Farmville and chatting on Facebook. The churning, noisy servers are stored on high shelves, because there are only two types of weather in Indonesia: extreme heat and extreme rain. By storing the servers just below the ceiling, the heat from the processors doesn't rise through the room, and if the room floods, everyone can keep on playing. In the wee hours of the morning, the cyber-cafés turn into informal black markets for buying and selling Zynga poker credits. One "broker" tells me he makes as much as $20,000 U.S. dollars per month roaming these cafés and peddling virtual chips between buyers and sellers all over town. Like Tencent and Giant Interactive in China, entrepreneurs in Indonesia are seeing that there is money to be made online if you can give people an easier way to pay.

Reports of how many Indonesians are online vary from 20 million to nearly 40 million, which is close to the size of Internet audiences in Brazil and India—both far more hyped markets. And that's just for accessing the Internet over computers. The mobile Web is huge in Indonesia, and BlackBerrys—not iPhones—are the hip device. You can You can buy BlackBerry data service by the day on prepaid phones, no contract required. For those who can't afford a BlackBerry, a local company called Nexian sells Qwerty-keyboard knockoffs from China for a fraction of the price, customized with Indonesian content like local bands and artists. In just a few years, Nexian has surged from a "nobody" to a company selling more than 5 million handsets per year, and eating into Nokia's market share. The Indonesian desire for keyboards—not touchscreens—isn't surprising given that the country's Web obsession is built on checking in, Tweeting, and messaging. Like so many other parts of the developing world, the Indonesian digital divide is being bridged with phones more than laptops, and Indonesians are doing it in a uniquely social way.

Yet unlike China, India, and even Israel, almost no Western Internet companies have sizable operations in Indonesia. Yahoo! is the closest, with a handful of employees that in 2010 started making offers to acquire small Indonesian homegrown properties on the sly. Arguably, there's no other Web audience in the world that is this huge and yet totally untargeted by Silicon Valley companies and venture capitalists. There are signs this will change dramatically in 2011; Google is already planning to open its first local office with Indonesian employees in the first quarter. Although that will likely change dramatically in the next few years.

But so far, that lack of Valley recognition has lead to a small, collegial cadre of several hundred Web entrepreneurs in Jakarta mostly finding each other on Twitter, creating their own community together through events organized by a local blogger named Rama Mamuaya. He's one of the only people who regularly writes about Jakarta's Internet scene, covering hundreds of tiny unknown companies and organizing regular meetups for thousands of Web enthusiasts trying to create sites explicitly for Indonesians.

Because Indonesia has had little hype, the community has grown organically—like the early days of the Valley and very unlike Web communities in Israel, India, and China that have been turbocharged by Western venture capital. The biggest reason Silicon Valley beat Boston as a venture capital and startup hot spot was that it was open culturally—trading employees, funding, mentorship, and ideas among competitors. It's not uncommon to see Web competitors in the Valley having dinner together and generally discussing business challenges, before they go back to the office for some late-night coding to bury one another in the market.

The same thing is happening in Indonesia's nascent Web scene. The competitive stakes are low, because right now funding opportunities and revenues are so small. Because they're creating the market opportunity as they go along, there's no feeling that the Web is a zero-sum game. They're all in this together.

For instance, the biggest problem they face is how to facilitate online payments in a country that lacks a strong system of national identification and where only 3 percent of the population has credit cards. The second largest problem is finding developers. In Indonesia, being an engineer is considered an entry-level position, not a lucrative career. Most companies have to invest six months or more in training the talent they need, making scaling up a challenge. But the more they all work together to build a Web ecosystem in Jakarta, the more it will become a hub for that kind of talent.

This generation grew up in a more connected world and mostly seem unfazed by all this colonial baggage that Tilaar and Ciputra's generation have had to work through. Yet, they feel a bond with the older generation of entrepreneurs, even if the older generation doesn't know who they are yet. Selina Limman, who is building a local review site called Urbanesia, said she'd seen Tilaar speak several times and found her inspirational. Mamuaya told me his dream was to meet Ciputra just once. "Did you get to see his house? I hear it's amazing," he said. That's important because the older generation of Indonesian moguls get things done in the country. SBY's critics say he's not the most decisive president, and his mission to weed out government corruption and bureaucracy will take time. Meanwhile, the younger generation of old Indonesian real estate, palm oil, and tobacco families are seed-funding the country's digital efforts. One ambitious company called IndoMog is aiming to solve the online payments problem. It has more than a dozen big national families and industrialists behind it—everyone from banks to Internet service providers to cyber-café owners to movie theatre moguls. The downside to building a company in Indonesia is that you need the buy-in of the older generation to make big changes, but the upside is that the older generation is surprisingly willing to invest. Indonesia is one of the only countries I visited where local entrepreneurs didn't complain about a lack of angel investors.

Solving the payment problem is the biggest issue if Indonesia is going to build its own thriving Web ecosystem. Right now, few of these Web companies are making any money. Indonesians do not want to pay for things online, so founders are loathe to follow the Chinese model of amassing a large number of micropayments to build a big company. "There is a big difference between one penny and free here," Leontinus Edison of online marketplace Tokopedia says. So most are following the Valley playbook of build now and monetize later. That may be a risky strategy: Encouraging the idea that the Web is free, rather than setting expectations that content and services cost money from the beginning. But the reticence is also practical. Few people have credit cards, and banks don't have a universal payment system that businesses can exploit.

Revenues from online advertising are more lucrative, even at this nascent stage. A lot of big brands are waking up to Indonesia's large, untapped market, and there aren't a lot of mass-media platforms on which to advertise. An online classifieds and message board site called Kaskus makes $50,000 a month in advertising, more than double what it takes to run the business. One reason costs are so low is the relative lack of big, lucrative coding jobs from the multinationals like Google, Yahoo!, and Microsoft and the lack of venture capital.

Mamuaya got a call from a Silicon Valley venture fund one day who asked him what the best Indonesian Web startup to put $1 million into would be. He replied, "None." Not because there aren't any promising startups, but because none of them need that much money. No one in this scene wastes their time trying to raise venture capital, because none of these companies are started with an expectation of it. A better approach for would-be investors might be an incubator. Mentorship is what this fledgling ecosystem really needs, but so far, that role is largely unfilled.

U.S. investors ignore Indonesia at their own risk. Other emerging markets that have developed faster than the island nation are not. On a flight between Indonesia and China, the plane had leaflets blaring "INVEST IN REMARKABLE INDONESIA" in each seat-back pocket, but a lot of the Chinese entrepreneurs I've met didn't need to be told. Richard Robinson says it's one of the hottest markets for his mobile games. India's SMSGupShup and a similar South African mobile social networking company called MixIt are both targeting Indonesia as well and already have millions of users with little effort. "It's not just an untapped market, it's a *juicy* untapped market," Robinson says. In Asian and African circles, Indonesia's rise to modernity and Web consumerism is a secret they want to keep from the United States.

Surprisingly, I've met more VCs visiting tiny Rwanda than juicy Indonesia. On the surface, Rwanda and Indonesia have little in common, but both are working to repair the psychological scars of colonialism, and both are relying on entrepreneurship for their futures.

Rwanda

10

Africa's Hottest and Riskiest Startup

I'm sitting in Jean de Dieu Kagabo's office on the second floor of his toilet paper manufacturing and packaging plant. He is so in tune with his company, SoftGroup, that he can sit at his desk, close his eyes, and hear if there's a problem with one of the machines downstairs.

He worked hard for those machines. When he was 18 he taught himself Mandarin and took the last of his family's money to China, to buy them. Many of the Chinese he encountered had never met an African before, but they'd heard of the Rwandan genocide. When he said where he was from, their expressions changed, and they'd say, "Ohhhhhhh! Hotel Rwanda!" One even gave him his seat on a bus in sympathy.

This office, which was once his father's when he ran a petrol company, is where Kagabo spends his days building his consumer package goods empire that supports his family now. The company makes straws, napkins, diapers, toothpaste, tomato paste, and other products people need every day, packaging them and selling them mostly in Rwanda, but also in Tanzania, Burundi, Uganda, and Kenya.

Kagabo is an exception to my rule that few great entrepreneurs were born rich. When his parents were still alive, Kagabo and his siblings were downright spoiled. His dad was a self-made man and always tried to instill a work ethic into his kids but to little avail. They groaned when forced to work summers at the petrol station. Indeed, even after the genocide, Kagabo's two older brothers spent more of the family's money partying rather than rebuilding the business. But all Kagabo does is work. He hits the Kigali club scene with his friends from time to time, but he doesn't date much. In Rwanda, dating quickly leads to marriage and then kids. Kagabo has two kids—his younger sisters. Until they are adults, he says he isn't free to start his own life.

Workwise, Kagabo is never content. He's grown the business from one product to fifteen, which he sells to roughly 70 large clients, including hotel chains, schools, hospitals, and mom-and-pop retailers. His formula is to make—or import in bulk and repackage—things that at least 50 percent of Rwandans use every day. The transportation costs of importing goods into tiny, landlocked Rwanda are huge, and taxes are levied on finished goods, driving costs up more. A bottle of Jack Daniels can cost up to $100 in Rwanda. But there are no taxes on raw materials.

It's not particularly rocket science, but by importing, say, huge drums of toothpaste and squeezing it into individual tubes, Kagabo can sell a product far cheaper than competing ones on the market and still make a 30 percent margin or greater on each product. He owns several German sports cars, wears smartly pressed shirts every day, owns a few houses, and is putting his two younger sisters through private school and planning their college educations. But none of this is enough.

Every Tuesday he goes to the markets and watches what everyday Rwandans are buying, how large of quantities they are buying, and what they are paying for these items. He grills them on whether they'd rather have a smaller size or a larger size or how much more they'd buy if the product was more affordable or packaged differently. This is how he discovered the potential gold mine of tomato paste—a staple of low-income Rwandan cooking.

He's plowing the returns from SoftGroup into other companies. Today he's showing me mock-ups for a $60 a night, Motel 6–style chain of hotels he wants to build near the airport. Indeed, there is a dearth of midpriced hotels in Kigali. Rwanda is being rebuilt from utter social, economic, and political devastation, and Kagabo sees a business idea around every corner.

Unfortunately, also around every corner are painful reminders of the worst hundred days of his life. Rwanda can be too small a country sometimes. Kagabo knows the name of the man who killed his father, and he knows that man died in jail a few years ago. He had never met him or confronted him and didn't want to. It was done, and he had to forgive and move on. But one day that man's son came to ask Kagabo for a job. The son had no idea his father had killed Kagabo's father, until it came out during the interview. The son left and never contacted him again. They still see each other on the street, and every time Kagabo gets a knot in his stomach. "I can't make small talk with him, I can't sit down and have a beer with him," he says. "I know I should be able to but I just can't."

But seeing this man is nothing compared to seeing people Kagabo actually watched commit brutal slayings. HIV-infected men who raped women and left them to die a slow, painful death. Hutu men who murdered their Tutsi wives and children. Teachers who turned over their Tutsi students to Hutu militias. Priests who killed the Tutsis that flocked to them for protection. Years after nearly a million corpses have been collected from the roadblocks and the clogged rivers, the bloodstains have been washed out of the churches and schools, what people like Kagabo saw still burns in their memories.

Friends of his who fled the country before the violence began know that all the movies, books, documentaries, and photographs they can see only add up to about 20 percent of what those like Kagabo who stayed behind witnessed. "People killing the babies in women's stomachs," he says, his expression one of someone who is far away in a very dark place. "Can you imagine? It's not even a person yet." Tears start to well up in his dark Rwandan eyes, he shakes himself back to 2009, and he says, "Let's talk about something else." Sitting at his father's desk, the head of his family at just 29, I can't bring myself to press him for more details about what he witnessed and how he escaped. I allow the subject to move back to toilet paper.

There's a constant debate in Rwanda over how much people should talk about the genocide. The policy is that no one is a Hutu or a Tutsi anymore, everyone is a Rwandan. The survivors try to walk a line between a near-impossible forgiveness and moving on, and yet, not letting the world forget what happened so it doesn't happen again. On every site where large groups were killed, there are wooden signs with painted black hands and the word "Jenoside." In some parts of the country, these signs crowd the sides of the road.

A tastefully done genocide museum traces the history of the violence, has cases of cleaned skulls of the victims and photos of children who died along with all-too-human descriptions of their favorite food, toy, best friend, and last words, if they're known. Other memorials are far harder to take. In Nyamata, you can visit several churches where Tutsis were killed, bloodstains remain, and in some cases scraps of clothing and bone are still there.

The Murambi Genocide Memorial, in the south of the country in Butare, is one of the most confronting. Butare was the height of the Rwandan intelligentsia before the genocide, and even after violence broke out, no one thought it could happen there. They were too sophisticated for such brutality. The prefect of the region was the only Tutsi prefect at the time. He welcomed refugees, and for two weeks, Butare was one of the only safe havens in the tiny nation. For a while, genocidaires also encouraged Tutsis to flock to Murambi for refuge, telling them they'd be safe in a newly constructed school on a hill. More than 40,000 Tutsis came and spent days huddled in the school without food or water. On April 19, genocidaires helicoptered in and threw grenades in the windows, shooting anyone who ran out of the building. Over three days more than 40,000 were killed and only a few people survived. Bodies were pushed into the natural ravines lining the school and covered up. When the French military came to assist the Hutu Power forces, they erected a volleyball court over one of the graves.

After the genocide, thousands of the bodies were exhumed, preserved in lime, and laid out on tables throughout the school. Emmanuel Murangira is the groundskeeper. He is one of only nine people who survived the massacre. His expression is hollow, his cheeks sunken and his forehead has a deep, scarred-over hole from a bullet that just barely missed its mark the day his entire family died. He lives in a sort of self-selected purgatory anesthetized with banana beer, living among these preserved corpses that he should have died with, but he says he can't leave his family and loved ones. He patrols the grounds like a ghost with a huge ring of keys, opening the rooms one by one and standing silently as you enter. The sting of lime burns your nose and eyes, preferable only to the sight of bodies twisted in horror, sometimes still clinging to one another with hair and clothing still intact.

My driver, Adam, is a genocide survivor. This was the first time Adam had visited Murambi, and he wandered through the hallways for a few minutes, then went out to the car to smoke a cigarette—a habit he picked up hiding out in the jungle with his brothers in April 1994. When he finally reemerged after the killing stopped, there were only three other kids left alive from his school, including one of his best friends today, Didier.

Didier hid out in his home during April, and miraculously his family was missed in the house-to-house killings. When he finally emerged, bodies were everywhere, and Adam was one of his only friends left alive. He has some photos on a CD-ROM and says if I want to see what really happened, not the sanitized version that documentaries and movies show, he'll show it to me. I'm trapped between my reporter instinct of wanting to understand what really happened and my human instinct of not wanting to know the depths of human evil. I say yes, but I never arrange to pick up the CD.

In Rwanda, genocide is even the sad undercurrent of funny stories. The week before I went to Murambi, Adam, Didier, and I were watching the fishing boats troll Lake Kivu for tilapia at sunset, and I was choking down my first bitter banana beer. In a few hours the fishermen would throw nets of fish on a nearby concrete slab, still flopping. They're gutted and grilled up to order, and once all the fish are gone, that slab turns into a dance floor for the locals.

Adam and Didier laughed, telling me about the trouble they got into in those years after the genocide. With just four kids left in their class after the genocide, the principal wound up drinking with them more than doing any teaching. But tragedy underlies every story. In a way they're past it, and in a way they never can be past it.

A National Trauma Survey by UNICEF in 1995 said that among children living in Rwanda during the genocide 99.9 percent of them witnessed violence, 79.9 percent experienced a death in their families, 69.5 percent saw someone killed or injured, most by machete, 31.4 percent witnessed rape or sexual assault, 87.5 percent saw dead bodies or parts of dead bodies, and 90.6 percent believed they would die.

The genocide comes up all the time in conversation in Rwanda, because it is entailed in the answer to so many basic conversational questions.

"How many brothers and sisters do you have?"
"How do you feel about the President?"
"Why did you leave Rwanda?"
"Why did you come back?"
"Why did you start your company?"
"Why don't you quit smoking?"

The more time you spend in the country, the less any of it makes sense. How it could have happened and how they can all live together side-by-side today with so much pain but so little violence is unfathomable. Buried deep in the heart of Africa, Rwanda is a study in the worst and the best in humanity.

෴

Time moves in funny ways in Rwanda. For centuries the Hutus, Tutsis, and the Twa lived together in harmony. But just 30 years of occupation by the Belgians changed the country forever. The Belgians favored the Tutsis because they looked more white. They deemed things like a thinner nose and taller, leaner physique as signs of intelligence.

Nearly 30 years of racist, preferential treatment lead to another 30 years of simmering tension between Hutus and Tutsis after independence, erupting in violence every few years. It culminated in a long-planned, organized campaign of Tutsi extermination that began in April 1994. A Hutu militia was trained, and a system of roadblocks was organized. Radio propaganda stoked the fires of hate, while songs and coded signs galvanized the Hutu majority. Genocide survivor Deogratias talks about going to medical school in Burundi and seeing classmates raise a hand to the top of the ear, make a fist, and raise it higher, saying in Kinyarwandan "at the level of the ear"—the place you were supposed to aim the machete when the killing started. At the time he thought they were friendly greetings, having no idea of the subtext.[1]

It was a long, thorough, plodding campaign that erupted at once when the Rwandan President Juvenal Habyarimana's plane was shot down in April 1994. Tutsis were blamed, and Rwanda erupted into one of the most brutal, horrifying genocides the world has ever seen. Over 100 days, nearly 1 million people were killed.

Many people believed that the World War II Holocaust could have never happened without the aid of technology—that people wouldn't have been able to kill that many people hand to hand. But in Rwanda, the rate of killing was nearly three times the rate of the Holocaust, and it was mostly done with machetes and clubs. Every tenth person in the population was killed. Author Philip Gourevitch calls it "the most efficient mass killing since the atomic bombings of Hiroshima and Nagasaki." An event nearly 60 years in the making would leave permanent scars in the country after just 100 days.

On one hand, Rwanda has made stunning progress in just 16 years since the genocide. There is almost no violent crime. Most of the country has access to water, basic health care, and primary school education. In the poorest areas of the country, almost all of the children have shoes. The worst road in Rwanda is better paved than the best road in the neighboring Democratic Republic of Congo. The land has been terraced to avoid erosion, subsistence farmers have been reorganized to focus on crops that their region grows best, and then they sell those crops at market, to buy everything else they need. Coffee and tea are new cash crops being exported around the world. Even in the neglected Twa, or Pygmy, tribes, the government is building spacious concrete houses—an upgrade from small mud huts. The Twa have been treated so horribly by both Tutsis and Hutus that they were initially suspicious and scared to move in, but they have finally started to. Throughout Rwanda, a large spray-painted "X" means a ramshackle house is coming down and a new one is going up.

Rwanda is getting connected to the world physically through a new railroad link from Tanzania but also virtually. Not only does Rwanda have four bars of cell phone reception even in the poorest, most mountainous areas, but throughout the countryside huge spools of fiber-optic cables line the roadside, while workers dig deep trenches. By the time this book is published, the entire country will be connected by high-speed fiber-optic lines—a boast the United States can't make. Rwanda has one of the more ambitious One Laptop Per Child programs, and already more than 100,000 school kids have the rugged bright green laptops, with plans to distribute them to half of its 2.5 million children in the next few years.

Government forms are increasingly processed online, and Nkubito Manzi Bakuramutsa, Rwanda's deputy CEO of the Development Board in charge of information technology, looks forward to a day when even the milking of cows is automated by technology. The Rwandan government sends 300 students at a time to the India Institute of Technology to learn hardware, software, and telecommunications engineering skills that can be applied in the tiny landlocked nation. To further facilitate this global connection, President Paul Kagame has mandated that the language of Rwandan schools be switched from French to English—a daunting challenge for a poor, resource-constrained nation, but one that will undeniably give it an advantage in Africa.

When it comes to electricity, the government has a $300 million deal with a U.S. energy company to tap trapped methane underneath Lake Kivu, which could explode if the methane is left alone. The methane is already powering southern regions of the country, and the hope is that it will become a sustainable power source for the next 40 years. Rwanda could potentially even export this cheap electricity to its neighbors, making money while preventing a natural disaster.

Radical moves like these are of huge importance. Economic prosperity for everyone is the best way to ensure the country doesn't fall back into genocide. And now, there are more mouths to feed. Following the fighting, Rwanda had a huge baby boom; the population soared 25 percent to nearly 10 million people. Anywhere you go in Rwanda, children come pouring out of the hillsides, bushes, and winding roads shouting "Mzungu!" or "white person." Unlike a lot of poor countries, they almost never beg. One child asked me for my water bottle, reaching out his hand and opening and closing it in a grabby motion, but his older brother pulled his arms down and told him they weren't supposed to beg. "That's a good boy!" Adam said, chuckling.

The baby boom was good in some ways, after one-tenth of the population was killed in the genocide. But tiny Rwanda is in danger of not being able to produce enough food to feed its burgeoning population. It needs to find some marketable skills fast. Kagame's model is Singapore—a tiny nation of just 5 million people with few natural resources that has a GDP of $181 billion. He's got a long way to go: Right now, Rwanda's GDP is just $4.5 billion. That's more than double what it was in 1998, but still tiny.

Sixteen years ago, Rwanda was written off as a place that would forever be mired in chaos and ethnic fighting. Today, by many accounts it's the cleanest, safest, and least corrupt African nation, but Rwanda is still incredibly poor—so poor that going jogging is considered a luxury in parts of the country because you are purposely expending calories just to stay thin. The gross national income per capita is less than half the rest of sub-Saharan Africa.

If Rwanda can be considered an African startup, President Kagame—the general of the army that defeated the genocidaires and took back over the country when the rest of the world did nothing—is the entrepreneur crafting it. Let's be clear: Kagame is a dictator, but most people I spoke with in Rwanda felt he was an overwhelmingly benevolent one. Foreign aid has flooded into Rwanda, making up half of the government's annual budget, and Kagame uses it like venture capital. His advisors have been people like former President Bill Clinton and Partners in Health founder Paul Farmer—giants on the Western political and aid stage. His managers are the local governors of each province, whom he grades harshly on a dozen or so measures from land terracing to education to litter to access to drinking water. If they don't perform, he fires them. The law bans plastic bags in Rwanda for litter and environmental reasons; they're even taken from you at the airport. The law requires people on mopeds to wear helmets and people in cars to wear seatbelts. Rwanda has a higher percentage of women in political office than any other country, and increasing women's rights post-genocide has been a priority for Kagame and the First Lady. Billboards are everywhere warning young boys and girls against accepting anything from "Shuga Mami" and "Shuga Dadi," or sugar mamas and sugar daddies. The billboards blare "SINIGURISHA," or "I am not for sale," and they always show an older, lecherous-looking person trying to give money, alcohol, or car rides to a younger person who is backing away with a resolute expression, holding up a finger or hand in protest. It's a message against prostitution, aimed at combating the spread of HIV, but it's also part of Kagame's consistent message that shortcuts and handouts aren't the way to get ahead. The three words even Kagame's critics use to describe Rwanda are safe, clean, and orderly.

Kagame hates that so much of the country runs on aid. "Why wouldn't you find it despicable to live in this situation?" Kagame said to author Stephen Kinzer. "Why should we be a country that depends on other people? What's wrong with us? Why do we live off other people's money, off the taxpayers of other countries? How can it be that people who lived in the country two hundred years ago were better off than we are today?"[2] But in the aftermath of the genocide, no one would actually invest in such a broken state, so he's using that aid to get the country to a point where they will.

It's important that those aid dollars go toward rebuilding the country, not lining pockets. Kagame has a zero tolerance policy on corruption. If someone gives a construction contract to his brother, he is put in jail. There's an audit done of government workers' homes—too many fancy objects, and they're investigated for taking bribes. Kagame even occasionally shows up at a restaurant to make his own health inspection. If food is stored on the floor or at suboptimal temperatures, he shuts down service right then and there—everyone out. As soon as you cross the boarder from chaotic Goma in the Democratic Republic of Congo and into the orderly beach town of Gisenyi, Rwanda, a big sign greets you that reads "INVESTMENT YES. CORRUPTION NO."

The order is more surprising when you consider that hundreds of thousands of genocidaires have already served their time in jail and have been reintegrated into society. Rwanda is one of few examples in history where the perpetrators of a genocide and the survivors and victim's families have gone back to live in the same intermingled towns and villages. The system for justice was called Gacaca and was based on an old tribal justice system of confession. The accused come before a village tribunal, and witnesses say what they saw; if the killers confess, they are given a light sentence, but they have to admit what they did to the people who suffered most. It's more about catharsis and facing the truth of what happened than it is about punishment. Kagame has admitted it's a system no one loves, and one that asks more of the survivors than the killers. Many Rwandans have described it to me as a flawed solution to an impossible problem. How do you bring millions of people to justice for killing a million of their neighbors and still have a country to rebuild?

International aid workers champion what Kagame has pulled off. Paul Farmer, of Partners in Health, calls him a great man. He moved his family to Rwanda, because of the support Kagame gave him in delivering health care to the poor. One Laptop Per Child founder Nicholas Negroponte told *Time*, "What is different about Rwanda is Paul Kagame's long-standing belief in us and us in him. We will walk to the end of the earth to help him and Rwanda. We want Rwanda to be a showcase."[3]

Kagame isn't a saint. As a general in a land of chaos, he's responsible for killing a lot of people. A 2010 United Nations report harshly criticized over-zealous retaliation by Kagame's troops in the genocide's immediate aftermath. And as the election for his second term approached, Kagame was criticized harshly by the foreign press for repressing political dissent. But most of the people I spoke with over two trips to Rwanda worried less about Kagame's repressive tendencies and more about who would replace him once his second—and, according to the country's constitution, last—term is up. It remains to be seen whether he'll do a power grab and stay in office or groom a successor. Either could have a detrimental effect on the country's stunning progress. Kagame told *The New Yorker* in 2009 that if he can't build a nation stable enough that he can pass the presidency onto someone else, then his Rwanda will have been "a failure."[4]

Kagame is frequently described as an angry man. He has lashed out at foreign critics, lambasting members of the international community for criticizing his lack of freedoms when they did nothing to help Rwanda when Kagame's family and countrypeople were being killed. "What freedoms are you teaching me if you can't take responsibility for the politics that killed one million people in Rwanda," he said, at an April 2010 commemoration ceremony for the genocide anniversary. He told Philip Gourevitch in 2009 that this annual address was a moment when he could, "spill out all of this anger. In politics or in diplomacy, you don't spill out the anger sufficiently. And that's why one time I said I wish I had another war, literally. The battlefield has a definition. It has very clear lines and even though it relies on tactics and strategy and bravery and so on, it provides a way to vent your anger and get it out. But managing these fluid situations and then the politics and the histories and the culture—fighting this in the way we do in modern times consumes a lot of energy and drives somebody crazy."[5]

It's easy to see why Kagame is angry. He grew up as a refugee in Uganda during the regular flare-ups of Hutu Power violence and, as the head of the Rwandan Patriotic Front (RPF), he was personally vilified and targeted in Hutu Power propaganda at the time. One newspaper in the genocide memorial shows an open grave with his name already on the tombstone, calling him a cockroach. Even still, when he came into power, he pioneered a policy of forgiveness in the country: giving dearmed Hutu militias positions in the RPF, giving Hutus their property back, and organizing the Gacaca tribunals.

The policy of forgiveness is hard for a lot of people in Rwanda to swallow. But some, like Kagabo, find strength in it. "The president explained we couldn't take revenge," he says. "Once you kill, what's the difference between you and him? We need them to build a country too. Killing isn't the punishment. It's not easy for me, but it's important. We can't let this happen again. The next generation needs to be free from it."

Rwanda is an entire country experiencing post-traumatic stress, but a country moving on nonetheless. Time moves in funny ways in Rwanda. No one could have imagined this much of the country could be rebuilt in just 16 years. But every April, it slows down just long enough for the nation to mourn—for all the memories that lie behind those eyes to overtake people. The survivors will never forget what they saw, and they'll never be okay with it. They can keep themselves from retaliating. They can move on, but that's the best they can do. They do it in hopes that they're the generation that finally breaks this Belgian curse some 50 years after independence. They feel acutely that the future of Rwanda rests on each of them, and the only thing Rwandans need as much as forgiveness is jobs.

⌘

Raj Rajendran didn't live in Rwanda during the genocide, and like a lot of people in the world, he was only somewhat aware that it was going on. After the genocide, a Ugandan investor that owned a Rwandan textile company recruited him to come fix it. Rajendran had been sort of a roving interim executive in a host of unsexy industries around the world, but when he got to Rwanda, he found a place unlike anywhere else he'd ever worked.

The company, Utexrwa, had been the largest manufacturing company in Rwanda before the genocide—an end-to-end manufacturing house making clothes and textiles from cotton and polyester fibers. When Rajendran arrived, the walls were bullet-ridden and crumbling, and only 300 of the original 1,000 staff members were still alive. Revenues had fallen from $20 million to $5 million.

The Ugandan investors wanted Rajendran to build Utexrwa back up so they could sell it. But, inspired by the country's strength, he wanted to rebuild Utexrwa into something that could give Rwandans good-paying jobs and make them proud. Despite winning contracts to make most of the government, military, prison, and school uniforms in Rwanda, he wasn't going to achieve success churning out the same cotton and polyester clothes that manufacturing houses in neighboring East African companies were making. He needed something innovative, something that could take what Rwanda had—which wasn't much—and turn it into something no one else had.

He started to wonder if it was silk. Rwanda seemed to have a similar climate to his home of India, and there was plenty of arable farm land—some 95 percent of the population were subsistence farmers. He imported some Japanese silkworms and started experimenting. The results were stunning: In China, the environment would support two growing cycles per year, and in India you could do five. In Rwanda, you could do ten. And a Parisian board had declared the quality of silk comparable to that of the finest silk producers in the world. More important for the country, the farmers growing the mulberry bushes that the worms munch on could make four times more money than they could growing coffee and tea—the closest Rwanda had gotten to premium internationally exportable products. Rajendran had essentially created a new natural resource for the country.

But just being able to harvest the silk and produce silk garments may not be enough. His Ugandan investors still want to sell the company, and Rajendran has been working to raise some buyout money so he can continue to build his dream. But the owners want more than most foreign investors have been willing, so far, to put into such a small market with such an unproven team. Rajendran could leave and start a new company, but that would mean buying all new equipment and hiring a whole new team. There's a big risk that Rajendran's dream dies or gets sold off on the cheap before it gets to the point he imagines, when he employs thousands of Rwandans, gives a better life to farmers, and even builds an elementary school on campus for his employees' kids.

The story underscores one of the endemic values Rwanda has. It's not necessarily the fertile soil and moderate climate, but rather that people who come here become so moved by what the country has been through and how much it has accomplished that they want to help. I was first brought to Rwanda by Dan Nova, a partner with Boston-based VC firm Highland Capital Partners. Nova has had a long, successful career investing in the tech boom of the late 1990s, and helping build Highland's Chinese and European practices. He was brought to Rwanda by Paul Farmer. In turn, Nova has brought several other Boston-based investors to Rwanda.

It's not uncommon for locals to see the Clintons, Tony Blair, Bono, or George Clooney in the country, they tell me. My husband and I traveled to see Rwanda's famous mountain gorillas, and we ran into Jack Hanna, the folksy animal expert who is well known for his appearances on *The Late Show with David Letterman*. It turned out Hanna had been coming to Rwanda since the genocide, helping the country develop its natural resources into top tourist destinations and also working closely with Kagame. On this occasion, Hanna had brought the descendents of the Von Trapps—yes, the ones *The Sound of Music* was based on—to sing at the annual gorilla-naming ceremony. They gave an impromptu concert and invited us to join them for dinner, but neither Hanna nor the Von Trapps were the focus of the dinner. The man everyone was there to see was named Frederick Ndabaramiye, and he had no arms.

In the aftermath of the genocide, 15-year-old Ndabaramiye was traveling on a bus near the Ugandan boarder, where many of the Hutu extremists had fled. Some guerilla fighters came down over the border and held the bus at gunpoint. They picked out Ndabaramiye and ordered him to kill all of the Tutsis on the bus.

He refused. They said they would kill him if he didn't. He refused again. So they tied him to a tree by the arms to watch while they killed all of the other passengers. Then they cut him down, threw him on the ground, and sliced off his arms just below the elbows, ignoring his pleas to leave him with at least a few fingers. They left him to bleed out and die.

Only, they accidentally left the ropes tied around his arms, and they worked like a tourniquet, saving his life. Eventually, some people found him, and Ndabaramiye—undeterred from living a life with no arms—learned to paint and play the guitar. The dinner was held in celebration of Ndabaramiye's new orphanage for genocide survivors. Ndabaramiye had been fitted with some prosthetics in the United States—a story covered by ABC News—but at dinner he took them off, saying some things were just easier to do with his own arms, such as they were. We watched in awe as he cut and ate food and drank a glass of red wine with ease.

Moved by Frederick's story, the family who hosted him in the United States was now back in Rwanda, helping him open the orphanage. An interior designer from San Francisco heard about Rwanda through them, and now he was here to help build some eco-lodges. And a couple from New York had joined in, here to help publicize the gorilla-naming ceremony over social media. When Hanna asked us to join them all for dinner, he said, "I could tell you love Rwanda, and that's why we're all here."

The staggering thing about Rwanda is its ability to lure in powerful, wealthy, or famous people, motivate them to want to build something for the country, and make them feel like the least important people in the room.

✑

But genocide guilt and personal connections aside, why should a Western audience care about tiny Rwanda? In part, because it's an example of aid working, turning an African country around dramatically in a short period of time. Collectively, Africa is the next huge sleeping giant only now waking up. For much of the 20th century, Africa's economy didn't grow, but in the early 2000s, the rate of growth more than doubled to 4.9 percent.

This wasn't all because of commodities like oil and minerals; many countries without resources grew just as fast. Today, with a $1.6 trillion collective GDP, Africa is equivalent to Brazil or Russia. It's expected to grow to $2.6 trillion by 2020. Consumer spending in Africa is $860 billion, which is expected to grow to $1.4 trillion by 2020. Approximately 128 million African households will become wealthy enough to have discretionary income by the same year. By 2030, 50 percent of them will be living in cities, and by 2040, 1.1 billion Africans will be of working age—the largest working-age population on the planet. Already the discretionary household spending there is larger than it is in India or Russia.[6]

Despite huge political, human rights, poverty, and health issues that still roil the continent, in pockets like Rwanda, real progress is being made. More people are safe, more people have access to jobs, and more African countries and companies are getting foreign investment, according to a 2010 McKinsey report that says, "Global business cannot afford to ignore the potential."[7] Structural changes in economies like lowering inflation, trimming debts, privatizing state-owned companies, cutting taxes, and strengthening legal systems have given birth to a nascent private sector where productivity is no longer declining; it is now rising nearly 3 percent annually since 2000. It has taken longer than other emerging economies, but Africa's middle class and urbanization is on the rise. Indeed, already Africa has a higher percentage of people living in cities than India does. That means incomes are rising faster. Foreign investors are paying attention: The flow of money into the continent has increased from $9 billion to $62 billion from 2000 to 2008.

Modern agriculture and mobile services may be the two most transformative opportunities: 60 percent of the world's total uncultivated, arable land is in Africa, and the continent added 316 million new mobile phone subscribers from 2000 to 2008.[8] One of the biggest mobile successes is M-Pesa in Kenya, a mobile banking product that reached nearly 40 percent of the adult population within two years of its launch and is the envy of much of the developing and developed world. In Kenya, you can pay for a cab by text message.

The challenge of Africa is the extreme fragmentation and diversity in language, quality of life, political systems, safety, corruption, and economic sophistication. Rwanda is considered a pre-transition economy in Africa—the most nascent with the lowest GDP per capita. But these economies—especially Rwanda—have some of the highest swings in growth. From 1990–2000 Rwanda's real GDP growth was a paltry .4 percent. From 2000 to 2008 it was 7.3 percent. In 2010, the World Bank named Rwanda the second-most-improved country in the last five years in terms of the ease of doing business; applauding the country's substantial and systemic policy changes.

Rwanda may be tiny, but if Kagame can move the educational system from French to English and continue to position the country as a clean, well-lit place to do business, it could become an unexpected continental hub for multinationals and foreign investors like Israel, Dubai or Singapore.

Sometimes, spending time in Rwanda makes me feel ashamed to be an American. While so many Rwandans I've gotten to know in the last two years were hiding out in jungles and under floorboards and their loved ones were being murdered, I was about to graduate from high school and obsessing over first-world problems like which college I would go to and who I would take to the prom. The day the killing started big, the tragic news in my world was that Kurt Cobain committed suicide, not that hundreds of thousands of Rwandans were being murdered.

Rwanda may still slip into this chaos again. But with fiber-optic cables rolled to every house and ubiquitous mobile phone access, it will be a lot harder to stifle what is happening. And if entrepreneurship—whether it's innovative new crops, manufacturing, or one of those kids with a laptop creating the Tencent of the African world—can lift people out of poverty, radical voices will have less sway.

Rwandans have something else going for them: hope. In many emerging markets, life is better than it was 16 years ago, but in Rwanda the juxtaposition may be the most staggering. Sixteen years ago, more than 90 percent of the children in Rwanda believed they would be killed. Today it may be authoritarian, but it is one of the cleanest, safest, and most organized countries in Africa. That remarkable change has given outsiders like Rajendran a reason to make Rwanda his home and survivors like Kagabo a reason to believe in his countrypeople again. As the economic miracle of Israel proved, sometimes a culture's ability to take risks, build something, and dream big are the most important natural resources a country can have.

Epilogue

Beyond Greed and Fear

$\mathscr{O}$ver a several-hour meeting in a thatched-roof snack bar in La Macarena, Colombian Commander BG Perez can barely get a sentence out without his phone ringing. He looks down, his face a mix of troubled and annoyed, hits the send-to-voicemail key, and continues what he was saying. It happens so frequently that I wonder why he doesn't just turn it off. But this is the least troubling and annoying part of his life in La Macarena—a daily struggle of ferreting out and beating back the last 4,000 or so paramilitary rebels in one of the remaining Revolutionary Armed Forces of Colombia (FARC) strongholds.

"Yesterday two youngsters came to me," he says to a U.S. State Department delegation in Spanish. "They said, 'General, take me out of here in a plane or I'm going to become a guerilla. I have no other option. My father will send me.'"

"What are you going to do once you get there?" Perez says he asked the boys. They shrugged. They had no idea. They just knew they needed to get out of La Macarena. "I took them," Perez continues. "My concern is it took a lot of courage to come up to me and have that conversation. How many others don't?"

You wouldn't know from this conversation how much success Perez and his colleagues have had over the last two years. More than 50,000 paramilitaries countrywide have demobilized, mostly voluntarily responding to radio messages telling them there was a way out, to just walk out, throw down their guns, and lift their arms and the state will take them in, give them legal help, and even provide job training. Two years ago Americans couldn't have traveled here. Today, we have an elaborate security detail, including snipers so stealthy we can't even see them, but we're not in cars with bulletproof windows. We're riding around in the open-air bed of the Colombian military's pickup trucks.

Perez estimates that about 4,000 FARC are left in the area, but they mix in the community in plain clothes, recruiting and pressuring locals to join the cause. The biggest reason they cave isn't political, he insists. The FARC has lost popular support in Colombia. But this region—isolated by mountains and lacking even a decent road to Bogotá—offers its citizens few other economic options, especially now that the Colombian government has cracked down on cocaine growing and trafficking, essentially killing the country's top export in the name of stability.

Alec Ross, the senior advisor on innovation for Secretary of State Hillary Clinton, was sitting across the table from Perez along with a small delegation from America's high-tech private sector. The State

Department is exploring a new strategy to take advantage of the tech community's support for the Obama administration to enlist small delegations of entrepreneurs, coders, digital do-gooders, and venture capitalists to give the United States fresh eyes on solving some of the world's problems. "America's greatest asset is our private sector," Ross says in a speech that it sounds like he's given a hundred times now. "If innovation is part of the hallmark of America, part of what we're trying to do is bring that to other nations."

We'd just been airlifted by the military into La Macarena and visited the John F. Kennedy School, a large open-air classroom on the edge of the jungle, where every child had a small, rugged laptop from the One Laptop Per Child program. At first glance, the rows of children in their uniforms and bright green-and-white computers was a stunning visual of the digital divide being bridged, until they told us the area didn't have Internet access, making all those computers a lot less useful.

But that problem was easy. Ross could fix things like that. He could make a call to the local telecom companies or throw some U.S. aid dollars at a mesh wireless network. But he couldn't create a high-growth economy for La Macarena. And he knew what Perez was describing was America's biggest threat in Colombia, the South American country that has gotten more American aid than any other.

The General's words would ring and nag in Ross's head for days. But now, he could offer little more than words of his own. "The United States wants to help you," he said. "We are proud of the work you've done here. We're well aware that something else has to come in once the military is done—that is the lesson we learned with Afghanistan. And you're close." The suited, all-American-looking state department official broke out in a semi-desperate smile as he said those last words. He had the resources of the world's largest superpower, the goodwill of Silicon Valley's tech community, and a few days later he'd be lavished with a glowing five-page profile in the *New York Times Magazine*. But at this moment, he felt utterly helpless.

This book began as a study in one thing: greed-based entrepreneurship in places emerging out of chaos and giving rise to
enormous greenfield opportunities the Western world no longer
has. The last thing I wanted to write was another book about global
politics or feel-good social entrepreneurship. But over the course
of my reporting, the topic of emerging market entrepreneurship
became too big to be about just greed and fear. After all, the last
few decades of the modern entrepreneurship movement in Silicon
Valley had been about more than just greed and fear. It was also
about the wonder of technology and making the world a better
place. It was about the ambition and ego and vision of a class of
founders who wanted to topple the status quo for fun, for money,
and for the little guy.

So, too, is the high-growth entrepreneurship wave sweeping the
developing world about more than just cash and stock options.
Marco Gomes wants anyone in Brazil to make money using the
Internet. Xu Xiong wants a way for anyone in China to get a driver's license without paying bribes. Ravi Ghate and Rajiv Mehrotra
want to connect India's villages to lifesaving information. Martha
Tilaar wants every Muslim woman to feel beautiful. And Jean de
Dieu Kagabo wants his once-decimated nation to stand on its own
two feet, consuming its own products and creating its own jobs.

Nearly 10 years after every Silicon Valley venture capitalist started
scouring China and India for the next billion-dollar idea, global
entrepreneurship has become a high-stakes game of survival. It's the
survival of the lucrative VC-to-IPO ecosystem that's provided hundreds of thousands of jobs and billions in returns. It's the survival
of the West's political interests in the world. And it's the actual survival of the billions of people in Asia, Africa, and South America
who finally have a way out of war, genocide, political oppression,
and slums.

High-impact entrepreneurship can do what aid, military inter-
vention, traditional diplomacy, and revolutions can't. Every country knows they want it. Every government can show you the

PowerPoint presentation arguing why it is a good investment. But how do they get it? And how does the West make sure it plays a role—whether motivated by purely financial issues, purely humanitarian issues, or a blend of the two?

As new superpowers emerge, America and Western Europe are in danger of being left out of shaping and profiting from this new world order unless we get on planes and listen to the people on the ground, those emerging middle classes we are trying to profit from. It has to be about more than the top of the pyramid or we lose out on the true promise of this stunning time in modern economic history. If Goldman Sachs is right, in 40 years, the United States will be the only member of the G7 nations that is still one of the seven largest economies in the world—and we won't be the biggest. Regardless of our own problems at home, the time is now to make sure we stay relevant in that new world, both politically and economically. This isn't a time for burying our heads, or we'll lift them up one day to see a world we don't recognize.

The emerging world is bigger than just India and China. Consider Indonesia—one of the largest countries in the world and one that China, India, Japan, and Singapore are investing in and profiting from more than Western investors are. Or, more striking, consider African markets like Rwanda—a place the world once failed. While Western aid is playing a large role in rebuilding the country, Dubai is providing the most for-profit investment, China is building its roads, and India is educating its new tech generation. There are even more countries rising up that this book didn't explore—like Russia, Mexico, Turkey, Nigeria, Kenya, and South Africa. As more of these economies achieve stability and seek to follow in China and India's footsteps, they're increasingly turning to other emerging markets for help, not the West.

Meanwhile, in the United States, a Russian company called Mail.ru Group has spent nearly $1 billion buying huge stakes in the hottest Silicon Valley up-and-comers like Facebook, social gaming site Zynga, and nouveau ecommerce company Groupon, while South African–based media conglomerate Naspers is buying stakes in the largest social media companies in emerging markets, like Tencent in China and BuscaPe, a huge comparison shopping engine running across hundreds of sites in Latin America. We used to assume that sophisticated Silicon Valley venture capitalists would be the dominant investors as high-growth entrepreneurship spread to the world, but just a decade or so in, that's not the case, even in our own country. In a world where technology has made talent and money this fungible, the incumbent advantage is almost gone.

It's a new paradoxical colliding world where statesmen act like entrepreneurs and investors, entrepreneurs and investors act like statesmen, and nonprofit leaders act like entrepreneurs, investors, and statesmen combined, laser-focused on revenues, profits, and a self-sustaining way to save the world without donors. It's a world where winning is an every-person-for-himself knife fight, but at the same time it's a world in which nations' selfish needs are best served by looking out for one another and giving newly secured nations a reason not to fall back into radicalism, despots, and coups. That reason isn't outsourcing. It's entrepreneurs starting globally competitive companies that do something better than anyone else in the world, or at least in their region and country.

While this may be a game with huge spoils—perhaps bigger than the global economy has seen before—it's economically a zero-sum game nonetheless. While the market opportunities of the rising middle classes in the developing world are so massive, many will win, but many more will lose trying to win. It's not a question of whether America will win—it's a question of which Americans will win, along with which Russians, Africans, Indians, Chinese, and South Americans. If the outsourcing decade of the 2000s was a new corporate-led version of imperialism, this is a new corporate-led world of diplomacy.

The approach to the emerging world shouldn't be fear, xenophobia, or defensiveness. The more that individual Westerners—and the Western world as a whole—accept, embrace, and cooperate with the rise, the more we benefit, at least politically. Because these entrepreneurs have an advantage: they get to start industries anew, and they have nothing to lose.

When Wences Casares goes back to the isolated sheep farm he grew up on in Patagonia, he has to stop on the way to load a truck with huge drums of kerosene that power the house. It takes the now-pampered millionaire back to a time when manual labor was the norm for him. Wrapping his fingers around the handles of the steel drums, he and his workmen brace themselves before lifting each one. But every once in a while, an empty drum is accidentally put in the wrong stack. When they lift it, it's so much lighter than they were expecting that it flies up in the air, almost comically. Having built companies in Argentina and Brazil before there were Spanish and Portuguese words for *entrepreneur*, Casares says lifting that empty drum is what it feels like starting a company in Silicon Valley now. "It's just so much easier," he says. He tells me this to explain why he's building his latest company in the Valley, not Latin America. But the flipside of the story is that Silicon Valley has become pampered, and that means certain entrepreneurial muscles are getting weaker.

The countries in this book—and many more in Asia, Eastern Europe, the Middle East, Africa, and South America—are as disparate as it's possible to be politically, economically, and culturally. But they all have one thing in common. It's not the state of their infrastructure, the quality of life, population, size, or any single industry or market opportunity. It's that the 20th century wasn't as good to them as it was to the West. Most of these countries spent the last 50 years fighting for independence and then fighting the harder, more uncertain internal battle for what their country stood for politically and culturally. They were consumed with finding their way as nations that gave their citizens basic rights like security and dignity, and in many ways, battling the ghosts left behind once occupying imperialist countries went home.

None is perfect, but that identity is solidifying, and security, political freedom, and economic opportunities are in aggregate growing. For these nations to continue to move forward, local entrepreneurs need to take over where government leaves off. Foreign investment needs to take the place of foreign aid. The 20th century may have been difficult for these countries, but the 21st century is theirs for the taking.

NOTES

1 Nothing to Lose

1. Janice E. Perlman, "Redemocratization Viewed from Below: Urban Poverty and Politics in Rio de Janeiro, 1968–2005," in Peter R. Kingstone and Timothy J. Power, eds., *Democratic Brazil Revisited* (Pittsburgh, PA: University of Pittsburgh Press, 2008), p. 265.
2. Jim O'Neill, "Building Better Global Economic BRICs," (New York: Goldman Sachs, November 30, 2001).
3. Jim O'Neill, "The N-11: More Than an Acronym," *BRICs and Beyond* (New York: Goldman Sachs, 2007), p. 140.
4. Paul Krugman, "The Big Zero," *The New York Times*, December 27, 2009.
5. Gary P. Pisano, "The U.S. is Outsourcing Away Its Competitive Edge," (Harvard Business Review Blogs, October 1, 2009).
6. Gary P. Pisano, "The U.S. is Outsourcing Away Its Competitive Edge," (Harvard Business Review Blogs, October 1, 2009).

2 The Death of Risk in America

1. Judy Estrin, *Closing the Innovation Gap: Reigniting the Spark of Creativity in a Global Economy* (New York: McGraw-Hill, 2009), p. 68.
2. Estrin, p. 72.
3. Estrin, p. 71.
4. Estrin, p. 67.
5. David Weild and Edward Kim, "A Wake-Up Call for America," (Grant Thornton, November 2009).
6. Estrin, p. 1.

3 How Israel Became a Startup Powerhouse

1. Dan Senor and Saul Singer, *Start-Up Nation: The Story of Israel's Economic Miracle* (New York: Twelve, 2009), p. 11–13.

2. Senor and Singer, p. 13.
3. Yannis Pierrakis and Stian Westlake, "Reshaping the UK Economy: The Role of Public Investment in Financing Growth" (London: NESTA, June 2009), p. 24.
4. Senor and Singer, p. 126.

4 Deng Xiaoping, for the Win

1. James Fallows, *Postcards from Tomorrow Square: Reports from China* (New York: Vintage Books, 2009), p. 32.
2. Leslie T. Chang, *Factory Girls: From Village to City in a Changing China* (New York: Spiegel & Grau, 2009), p. 12.
3. Chang, p. 12.
4. Chang, p. 13.

5 Revenge of the Copycats

1. Sherman So and J. Christopher Westland, *Red Wired: China's Internet Revolution* (London: Marshall Cavendish Business, 2010), p. 116.

6 India's Invisible Infrastructure

1. Edward Luce, *In Spite of the Gods: The Rise of Modern India* (New York: Anchor Books, 2006), p. 330.
2. Luce, p. 277.
3. Vivek Wadhwa, "Foreign-Born Entrepreneurs: An Underestimated American Resource," *Kauffman Thoughtbook 2009* (Kansas City: Ewing Marion Kauffman Foundation, 2008) p. 178.
4. Vivek Wadhwa, "A Fix for Discrimination: Follow the Indian Trails," Techcrunch.com, February 21, 2010.
5. Fareed Zakaria, *The Post-American World* (New York: W.W. Norton & Co., 2008) p. 189.
6. Luce, p. 48.
7. Luce, p. 49.

7 India's Mighty Microeconomy

1. Edward Luce, *In Spite of the Gods: The Rise of Modern India* (New York: Anchor Books, 2006), p. 9.

8 Do You Know Who You Are Talking To?

1. Alberto Carlos Almeida, "Core Values, Education, and Democracy: An Empirical Tour of DeMatta's Brazil," *Democratic Brazil Revisited*, p. 235.
2. Michael Reid, *Forgotten Continent: The Battle for Latin America's Soul* (New Haven, CT: Yale UniversityPress, 2007), p. 17.
3. Jonathan Wheatley, "Dancing through the Economic Crisis," *Financial Times*, July 6, 2009.
4. Michael Skapinker, "Brazil Is the 21st-Century Power to Watch," *Financial Times*, October 29, 2009.
5. Peter R. Kingstone and Timothy J. Power, eds., *Democratic Brazil Revisited* (Pittsburgh, PA: University of Pittsburgh Press, 2008), p. 2.
6. "Food, Glorious Food: Agricultural Commodities," *BRICs and Beyond*, p. 265.
7. Jonathan Wheatley, "Dancing Through the Economic Crisis," *Financial Times*, July 6, 2009.

9 The Emerging World's Big Secret

1. Joe Studwell, *Asian Godfathers: Money and Power in Hong Kong and Southeast Asia* (New York: Atlantic Monthly Press, 2007), p. 105.
2. Studwell, p. 105.
3. Studwell, p. 107.
4. Studwell, p. 137.
5. Adrian Vickers, *A History of Modern Indonesia* (Cambridge, UK: Cambridge University Press, 2005) p. 223.
6. Studwell, p. 184.
7. Studwell, p. 184.
8. Studwell, p. 184.

10 Africa's Hottest and Riskiest Startup

1. Tracy Kidder, *Strength in What Remains: A Journey of Remembrance and Forgiveness* (New York: Random House, 2009) p. 96.
2. Stephen Kinzer, *A Thousand Hills* (Hoboken, NJ: Wiley, 2008) p. xvi.
3. Nick Wadhams, "Can One Laptop Per Child Transform Rwanda's Economy?," *Time*, June 18, 2010.
4. Philip Gourevitch, A Reporter at Large [column], "The Life After," *The New Yorker*, May 3, 2009, p. 38.
5. Gourevitch, p. 37.
6. "Lions on the Move: The Progress and Potential of African Economies" (New York: McKinsey Global Institute, 2010) p. 3–4.
7. "Lions on the Move," p. 1.
8. "Lions on the Move," p. 22.

AUTHOR'S NOTE

This book was the result of roughly 40 weeks of on-the-ground reporting in 11 different countries around the world, principally China, India, Israel, Brazil, Rwanda, and Indonesia. From mid-2008 to mid-2010, I met with hundreds of entrepreneurs in these countries, dozens of local investors, aid workers, policy makers, and everyday locals consuming these companies' products in their burgeoning home markets. Many of the entrepreneurs in this book did not speak English, and I relied heavily on local translators to interview them. Unless stated otherwise, every quote in this book came from a first person interview, in country.

It's impossible to know everything about a country in a few visits, so I've also relied heavily on analyst and research reports and several dozen excellent books on business, politics, economics, and history of the various countries I visited, many of which are cited in the endnotes. This book is meant to capture the entrepreneurial spirit, challenges, and opportunities at this extraordinary moment in economic history, reflected through what I saw and the hundreds of locals I met.

The Kauffman Foundation gave me a generous grant to help with the expenses of reporting this book, helping to make the project possible.

INDEX